HIS GRACE

AND OTHER ESSAYS

BY

REV. DAVID E. CLARKE

The Bible used in this book is from the NKJV.

This book was printed in the United States of America.

To order additional copies of this book, contact:

Rev. David E. Clarke
P.O. 82
Ashville, Ohio 43103

Published by FWB Publications
Columbus, Ohio

FWB

Rev. David E. Clarke

OTHER WORKS BY REV. CLARKE:

Eclectic Essays

The Prince and the Four Gardens

The Valley Where Strangeness Occurs

A Mighty Tree

The Little Book of Longer Poems

Songs without Music and Other Poems

Concerning the Christ

Thy Kingdom Come: Day One

DEDICATION

This book is dedicated to my family and friends

To those who may read these words

And to my Lord and Savior Jesus Christ

HO KURIOS MOU KAI HO THEOS MOU

TABLE OF CONTENTS

ACKNOWLEDGEMENTS

I wish to thank those many folk, both family and friends, who contribute and aid and add to my work and my life.

My thanks are given and extended to Steve and Becki Matzenbach for our new friendship and their art and talent. Thank you Becki for the three new charts you have crafted and are given in this work.

PREFACE

"His Grace, and Other Essays," is a short work with a simple purpose in mind. I have attempted to contribute to the discussion concerning six central questions asked by millions of seekers and Christians. Six important and basic questions Christians ask. Who is God? How is His demonstration of Himself as a Trinity to be understood? How should and can a seeker and student of the Word read the Holy Bible? What and how is a person able to find salvation? What is the doctrine of sanctification and how is it given and manifested in the Christian's life? What is faith? How is the Lord's grace given and demonstrated in our lives?

The first five essays have been reoffered from my previous work, "Concerning the Christ." They have been reordered and offered as a starting answer for those who may have thoughts and questions concerning these various topics. They are offered as beginning steps on a seeker's journey to find answers to these questions. They are not meant to be exhaustive. How could they be? I am just a seeker myself. I am just a person travelling and living in the tent of mortality and have not made it to where I am further clothed in the habitation of His holiness and eternity. I am not complete yet, but I offer my thoughts concerning these weighty matters and topics. The answers offered have given to me a certain peace and completeness of thought in these matters of importance to all of us.

The sixth essay, <u>His Grace</u>, is a new work concerning the debate between the Predestinarian and the Free-will segments within the Christian community. I hold and offer a capatabilistic approach to this highly divisive issue. I believe totally that this argument is not an either/or understanding, but indeed is a both/and understanding. I submit my paradigm in light of my understanding of this issue.

I have included as an appendix certain charts concerning these various essays and points of view which have aided my understanding in these matters.

My goal and purpose is to add some information to the seeker to help our communal understanding.

God bless the reader of this work.

THE TRINITY[1]
HOLY, HOLY, HOLY! LORD GOD ALMIGHTY

Holy, Holy, Holy! Lord God Almighty
Early in the morning
Our song shall rise to Thee
Holy, Holy, Holy! Merciful and mighty!
God in three Persons, blessed Trinity!

Holy, Holy, Holy! All the saints adore Thee,
Casting down their golden crowns
Around the glassy sea;
Cherubim, and seraphim falling down before Thee,
Which wert, and art, and evermore shall be.

Holy, Holy, Holy! Tho' the darkness hide Thee,
Tho' the eye of sinful man
Thy glory may not see;
Only Thou art Holy – there is none beside Thee
Perfect in pow'r, in love, in purity.

Holy, Holy, Holy! Lord God Almighty
All Thy works shall praise Thy name
In earth, and sky, and sea.
Holy, Holy Holy! Merciful and mighty!
God in three Persons blessed Trinity![2]

-Reginald Heber and John B. Dykes

---

[1] This Chapter, The Trinity, was originally published as, "The Trinity and the Convergence of Worship," in my earlier work, "Concerning the Christ," Published by FWB Publishing, c. 2011.
[2] Words by Reginald Heber written 1826. Music by John B. Dykes written 1861.

THE TRINITY

The perfection in the unity, in the diversity, in the community of the Trinity[3]

How to worship a God such as our God? A God so benevolent and wonderful and gracious He has decided to reconcile fallen mankind back to Himself via Himself. A God who is a triune God, a Trinity. This point baffles and mystifies all of us in its complexity and manifestation. A Trinity who many define incorrectly as three. A Trinity who others just as incorrectly define as one. In reality, They are a Tri-unity, three in one. The great mystery of our God is the unveiling of His plan of reconciliation in the revelation and offices of God the Father, God the Son and God the Spirit. The Apostle Paul in 1 Corinthians 13 through the inspiration of one of the Trinity, God the Spirit has written that we, while in our mortality, gaze into a mirror obscurely, through a glass darkly. We define things and persons beyond and apart from us, beyond the physical, mortal and empirical through eyes obscured and darken through our veil of mortality. We know in part. We see in part. We understand in part. This situation will not always be the case, re. 1 John 3:2, but it is the norm for now. A person or organization who presents a hypothesis or premise as total and complete and without any potential for future refinement or knowledge is not presenting a hypothesis in a completely truthful manner. From the highest of stations to the lowest of stations, we all see through mortal eyes. From the greatest of minds and understanding to the dimmest of understanding, we all see into that dark mirror obscurely.

---

[3] Dr. Ravi Zacharias, RZIM, Norcross, Georgia.

God has chosen in His divinity, sovereignty, holiness, infinitude, immutableness and love to present and reveal Himself in the manner and to the degree He has chosen. He has given to us graciously what we need to have both in His word and His Spirit. He has chosen to reveal Himself in three offices or persons of Deity: the Father and the Son and the Holy Spirit. We must worship our God in His revelation that He has given to us. The Trinity is not three outside the one nor is it one. It is three within the one. To repeat Dr. Ravi Zacharias' description given at the introduction of this essay, 'the Trinity is the perfection in the unity, in the diversity, in the community of the Trinity'. What a marvelous description of our God and Lord! The Trinity is the completion in the oneness in the various manifestations in harmony with each other. Our Triune God is defined as the union of the Father, Son and Holy Spirit in one Godhead. The Godhead, the essential being of God is God's divine nature.

How to worship such a God as we have? God the Father, the singularity of all. The creator and the sovereign. Within Himself, all things and creatures have and owe their existence. He is because He is and we are because He is. I am reminded of the five attributes ascribed to God by the writer A.W. Tozer mentioned throughout this work: He is sovereign. He is immutable. He is love. He is holy. He is infinite. Of course, these attributes describe the Son and the Spirit as well. For within the Trinity, there is one other attribute: *Harmony.*

In this day of self-aggrandizement, within the existentialism and experientialism and pietistic behaviorism and the other versions of the Christian selfish, 'me, me, me' as a community we have forgotten we are called to be a community. Our disharmony does not reflect the harmony of God. The modern church has forgotten that the historic Christ, and existential Christ of today, the Word of Scripture of John 1 and the Holy Spirit, the second *parakletos,* the second comforter of John 14 must be found in harmony. Too many paths and diversions from secular humanism and liberalism and Hegelism and the other isms and schisms have diverted the walk and altered the talk of what the Apostle Paul wrote to the church of Corinth, "Christ and Christ crucified." With each passing year and the inevitable new thesis, Christianity finds a wider and wider gorge separating us from the gospel message that God has decreed for us. But His gospel message is clear. He, the Christ died on that cross. He, the Christ was buried in holiness in a borrowed tomb. He, the Christ rose again the third day the Firstfruits of God.

Why this gospel? God in that determinate council written of in Acts 2 chose to pay for the redemption of fallen man back to Himself through the shedding the blood of God the Son. It is God's plan. We read of this plan and the process of redemption and reconciliation in the Apostle Paul's letter, 1 Corinthians 15:22-28:

> **For as in Adam all die, even so in Christ all shall be made alive. But each one in his own order: Christ the first fruits, afterward those who are Christ's at His coming. Then comes the end, when He delivers the kingdom to God the Father, when He puts an end to all rule and all authority and power. For He must reign till He has put all enemies under His feet. The last enemy that will be destroyed is death. For "He has put all things under His feet." But when He says "all things are put under Him," it**

is evident that He who put all things under Him is accepted. Now when all things are made subject to Him, then the Son Himself will also be subject to Him who put all things under Him that God may be all in all.[4]

God's process cited above in a short synopsis is consistent with all of the Old Testament covenant promises from Adam to Abraham and all of his heirs. This process is consistent with Old Testament prophecy, the Jerusalem church of the Jewish disciples of the Lord, the Messiah, God the Son, Jesus Christ. This process is consistent with the dispensational truths revealed to Paul concerning the garnering of the bride of Christ in this age of grace. This process is consistent with the revelation of the Lord penned by John the Revelator in the future 70th week of Daniel we call the Great Tribulation. The Christ arose as the First-fruits. Then His bride and His kingdom. He reigns sovereign and all is overcome by Him via either acceptance or rejection. The Christ, the Lord, the God-man, God the Son will be the successful method and manner of reconciliation of a lost, dying, separated mankind back to God. God has a plan.

God the Son came as a man. How to worship such a God as this? Throughout history and time, mankind has reached high to be a god and be god-like. At a particular moment in time some two thousand years ago, God the Son lowered Himself to be someone that was beneath Him. Would we lower our humanity and humanness to be the saving propitiation for an earthworm? Would we abase

---

[4] All Scripture cited in this work unless otherwise referenced are from the New King James Version of the Holy Bible.

ourselves to bring salvation to a germ? When we speak of the kenosis (from the Greek: *kenoo*[5] Phil. 2:7), the emptying out, the divestiture of the Lord when He put upon Himself humanity, to me that is what we are saying. We read of this in Paul's letter, Colossians 1:13-23:

> **He has delivered us from the power of darkness and conveyed us into the kingdom of the Son of His love, in whom we have redemption through His blood, the forgiveness of sins. He is the image of the invisible God, the firstborn over all creation. For by Him all things were created that are in heaven and that are on earth, visible and invisible, whether thrones or dominions or principalities or powers. All things were created through Him and for Him. And He is before all things, and in Him all things consist. And He is the head of the body, the church, who is the beginning, the firstborn from the dead, that in all things He may have the preeminence, For it pleased the Father that in Him all the fullness should dwell, and by Him to reconcile all things to Himself, by Him, whether things on earth or things in heaven, having made peace through the blood of His cross. And you, who once were alienated and enemies in your mind by wicked works, yet now He has reconciled in the body of His flesh through death, to present you holy, and blameless and above reproach in His sight – if indeed you continue in the faith, grounded and steadfast, and are not moved away from the hope of the gospel which you heard, which was**

---

[5] All words not in English will be italicized as also words to indicate emphasis or for clarity.

> preached to every creature under heaven, of which
> I, Paul, became a minister.

Paul continues in 2:9-10:

> For in Him dwells all the fullness of the Godhead
> bodily; and you are complete in Him, who is the
> head of all principality and power.

God the Son. God the creator. God the method of our salvation. Our Lord Jesus Christ is the person of the Godhead you can shake hands with. "For in Him dwells all the fullness of the Godhead bodily . . ." As the Holy Spirit is our second comforter, the Messiah is our first comforter and advocate, the first *parakletos* in the Greek. Like the Father in that blessed harmony of the Trinity, the Christ is the singularity of the focus and completion of all truth, His truth and experience and existence. All before is but a shadow or image pointing toward Him and all after is but a pale definition or reflection of the truth if not found completed in Him and His sacrifice to redeem mankind.

God the Spirit, the second *parakletos*, the second comforter. How to worship such a God as this? He is our educator and our seal and our guarantee of what God has done and who God is to those who serve Him. Paul writes in Romans 8:1-11:

> There is therefore now no condemnation *(we are
> not guilty in God's judgment)* to those who are in
> Christ Jesus *(those who are believers)*, who do not
> walk according to the flesh, but according to the
> Spirit. For the law of the Spirit of life *(His gracious
> salvation to us)* in Christ Jesus has made me free

from the law of sin *(the Mosaic Law)* and death *(our adamic nature)*. For what the law *(the Mosaic Law)* could not do in that it was weak through the flesh, God did by sending His own Son in the likeness of sinful flesh *(the Kenosis, the incarnation of God the Son, the divestiture)*, on account of sin: He condemned sin in the flesh *(at Calvary and His resurrection)*, <u>that the righteous requirement of the law might be fulfilled in us</u> *(God the Son has paid the price)* who do not walk according to the flesh but according to the Spirit. For those who live according to the flesh set their minds on the things of the flesh, but those who live according to the Spirit, the things of the Spirit. For to be carnally minded *(worldly minded)* is death *(separation from God)*, but to be spiritually minded is life and peace *(reconciliation and harmony with God)*. Because the carnal mind is enmity *(mutual hostility)* against God; for it is not subject to the law of God, nor indeed can be. So then, those who are in the flesh cannot please God. But you are not in the flesh <u>but in the Spirit, if indeed the Spirit of God dwells in you. Now if anyone does not have the Spirit of Christ, he is not His. And if Christ is in you,</u> the <u>body is dead because of sin, but the Spirit is life because of righteousness</u> *(God's righteousness)*. <u>But if the Spirit</u> *(God the Spirit)* <u>of Him</u> *(God the Father)* <u>who raised Jesus</u> *(God the Son)* <u>from the dead dwells in you, He</u> *(God the Father)* <u>who raised Christ</u> *(God the Son)* <u>from the dead will also give life to your mortal bodies through His Spirit</u> *(God the Spirit)* <u>who dwells in you.</u> *(Without the Spirit, we are not Christian believers and therefore this indwelling must happen upon conversion.)*

God, the Triune God, in harmony has a plan for all of mankind to be reconciled, to be saved. My, oh my, what a God we serve! Who is like our God? We are and can only be saved through the death, burial and resurrection of God the Son, the Lord and Savior Jesus Christ. As believers, we are only made and considered righteous and worthy through the applying to us God's righteousness. It could never be our baptisms and works. It could never be by this or that or whatever we have chosen to add to His work at Calvary over the last two thousand years in violation of Galatians 6:14, "But God forbid that I should boast except in the cross of our Lord Jesus Christ, by whom the world has been crucified to me, and I to the world." Only by His Gospel. Only by His Cross. Only by His burial. Only by His resurrection do we have access into this mysterious and wonderful reconciliation with a sovereign, holy, immutable, loving and infinite God. This triune God. Who to worship such a God as this?

C.S. Lewis writes in his wonderful apologetic, "Mere Christianity" of this Trinity:

> . . . In the Christian life you are not usually looking at Him. He is always acting through you. If you think of the Father as something 'out there', in front of you, and of the Son as someone standing at your side, helping you to pray, trying to turn you into another son, then you have to think of the third Person as something inside you, or behind you
> . . . The whole dance, or drama, or pattern of this three – Personal life is to be played out in each one of us: or (putting it the other way round) each one of us   has got to enter that pattern, take his place

in that dance . . . If you want to get warm you must stand near the fire: if you want to be wet you must get into the water. If you want joy, power, peace, eternal life, you must get close to, or even into, the thing that has them. They are not a sort of prize which God could, if He chose, just hand out to anyone. They are a great fountain of energy and beauty spurting up at the very center of reality. If you are close to it, the spray will wet you: if you are not, you will remain dry. Once a man is united to God, how could he not live forever? Once a man is separated from God, what can he do but wither and die? But how is he to be united to God? How is it possible for us to be taken into the three – Personal life? You remember what I said in chapter I about *begetting* and *making*. We are not begotten by God, we are only made by Him: in our natural state we are not sons of God, only (so to speak) statues.

We have not got *Zoe* or spiritual life: only *Bios* or biological life which is presently going to run down and die.   Now the whole offer which Christianity makes is this: that we can, if we let God have His way, come to share in the life of Christ. If we do, we shall then be sharing a life which was begotten, not made, which always has existed and always will exist. Christ is the Son of God. If we share in this kind of life we also shall be sons of God. We shall love the Father as He does and the Holy Ghost will   arise in us. He came to this world and became a man in order to spread to other men the kind of life   He has – by what I call 'good infection'. Every Christian is to become a little Christ. The whole purpose of becoming a Christian is simply nothing else. . . . It is just this; that the business of becoming a son of God, of being turned from a created thing into a begotten thing, of passing over from the temporary biological life into timeless 'spiritual' life has been done for us. . . . If we will only lay ourselves open to the one Man in whom it was fully present, and who, in spite of being God, is also a real man, He will do it in us and for us. Remember what I said about 'good infection'? One of our own race has this new life: if we get close to Him we shall catch it from Him. Of course, you can express this in all sorts of different ways. You can say that Christ died for our sins. You may say that the Father has forgiven us because Christ has done for us what we ought to have done. You may say that we are washed in the blood of the Lamb. You may say that Christ has defeated death. They are all true. . . .[6]

This is a demonstration of the harmony of the Trinity and to paraphrase Lewis, God is in us (God the Spirit) and beside us (God the Son) and is before us as our goal and destination and sovereign (God the Father).

God the Spirit inside us. The second comforter, who leads, guides and educates us to make us chaste and fit to be the bride of the Lord. God the Spirit, our seal and guarantee. To paraphrase William Barclay: the Holy Spirit is the little bit of God that we get until we receive all of God.

---

[6] Clives Staples Lewis, Mere Christianity, (C.S. Lewis Pte. Ltd. Copyright 1980.) pp. 176, 177, 181 & 182. One should read of Book 4 in Lewis', Mere Christianity on this subject of the Trinity.

I like the Apostle Paul's description inspired by this same God the Spirit in his letter to the Ephesians 1:13-14:

> **In Him you also trusted, after you heard the word of truth, the gospel of your salvation; in whom also, having believed, you were sealed with the Holy Spirit of promise, who is the <u>guarantee</u> of our inheritance until the redemption of the purchased possession, to the praise of His glory.**

The Greek word we translate here as 'guarantee' is *arrabon* and means a pledge or promise. In Modern Greek, the word can be translated engagement ring. We, when we are saved, are given to wear in and on our hearts, God's engagement ring, God the Spirit until we are married to the Lord, God the Son as the Marriage Supper of the Lamb.

God the Son beside us. The first comforter: our method and manner of salvation, our propitiation and redemption and justification. He is all we can ever become or necessary to receive in the eternal sense. In a remarkable narrative of our great God, Paul writes in Ephesians 1:3-14:

> **Blessed be the God and Father of our Lord Jesus Christ, who has blessed us with every spiritual blessing in the heavenly places in Christ *(God the Son)*, just as He *(God the Father)* chose us in Him *(God the Son)* before the foundation of the world, that we should be holy and without blame before Him *(God the Father)* in love, having predestined us to adoption as sons by Jesus Christ *(God the Son)* to Himself *(God the Father)*, according to the good pleasure of His will *(God the Father)*, to the praise**

of the glory of His grace *(God the Father's gift, God the Son)*, by which He *(God the Father)* made us accepted in the Beloved *(God the Son)*. In Him *(God the Son)*, the forgiveness of sins, according to the riches of His grace *(God the Son)* which He *(God the Father)* made to abound toward us in all wisdom and prudence, having made known to Us the mystery of His will *(God the Father)*, according to His *(God the Father)* good pleasure which He *(God the Father)* purposed in Himself *(God the Father)* that in the dispensation of the fullness of the times He *(God the Father)* might gather together one all things in Christ *(God the Son)*, both which are in heaven and which are on earth – in Him *(God the Son)*. In Him *(God the Son)* also have obtained an inheritance, being predestined according to the purpose of Him *(God the Father)* who works all things according to the counsel of His will *(The Triune God)*, which we who first trusted in Christ *(God the Son)* you also trusted, after you heard the word of truth, the gospel of your salvation; in whom also, having believed, you were sealed with the Holy Spirit *(God the Spirit)* of promise, who is the   guarantee of our inheritance until the redemption of the purchased possession, to the praise of His glory *(the Triune God)*.

The above passage is a wonderful and mighty demonstration of the interworking harmonious working of the Triune God and the instrumentality of the finished work of the cross by God the Son, Jesus our Savior.

God the Father is our goal and destination. The third Person of this Trinity. He is sovereign, immutable, holy, loving and infinite as are God the Son and God the Spirit. He is the totality of all things re. I Corinthians 15: 23-28. He is not disjointed or disconnected from the Son and the Spirit, but He has described Himself in a personal sense, as all three are, to afford a limited and finite mortal mankind a glimpse of Himself, the divine God. I quoted Dr. Ravi Zacharias earlier in this chapter concerning the nature of the Trinity and it bears repeating, "The perfection in the unity, in the diversity, in the community of the Trinity." What a God we serve! How to worship such a God as this?

GOD'S PLAN

When we needed a saving plan
God the Father sent us a Man
Not a mortal king to assume a mortal throne
But the King of kings to give us a home

When we needed a strong plan
God the Son allows us to stand
He makes us just, established and free
He redeems His creation and even me

When we needed a guiding plan
God the Son heads His band
From a manger low to His Father's side
He will provide and in Him we abide

When we needed an enlightening plan
God the Spirit will help us understand
We may toss and turn in this finite
He will teach and give us insight

When we needed an encouraging plan
God the Spirit will hold our hand
Though the sinful prince assails all the day
The Lord will give peace; the Spirit will help us pray

When we need a saving plan
God the Son sent Himself as the blameless Lamb
God loves us so much that we not suffer loss
God the Father gave the Dove to carry our sin's cross.

-David E. Clarke 7-1993

THE CONVERGENCE OF WORSHIP

PSALMS 22:1-5

My God, My God, why have You forsaken Me?
Why are You so far from helping Me,
And from the words of My groaning?
O My God, I cry in the daytime, but You do not hear;
And in the night season, and am not silent.
But You are holy, enthroned in the praises of Israel.
Our fathers trusted in You;
They trusted, and You delivered them.
They cried to You, and were delivered;
They trusted in You, and were not ashamed.

God is holy and sits upon His throne in the presence of praises to His name. Psalms 22, a Messianic Psalm reveals a marvelous truth concerning our holy sovereign Triune God. He sits on His throne in the presence of our praises. He inhabits and dwells in our praises. The Tabernacle of Moses and David, the Temples of Solomon and Zerubbabel, the Temple of the Holy Spirit, the believers of the grace of God in this age of grace are all meant to be the habitation and throne of the almighty God. As such the Lord God is to be surrounded by our worship and our praise. Today the church seems to have only partially clothed and surrounded His throne. Praise is much more that a song or a testimony. Praise is the active participation of the body of Christ, the church in glorifying Him as we become the bride of Christ. Praise is of course a song and a testimony, but it can also be a can of corn or some other food or drink given to a mission. Praise and worship is coming to a church service or working in a mission to be the hands and feet of the Lord in this age of grace. Praise and worship can be the giving of a kind word in the Lord's name, etc. . . . . It is the placing aside of ourselves and giving the preeminence to our God. In becoming more like Him in our imitation of the Lord, 1 Corinthians 11:1, we become more a light to a dark and dying world. In our praise and worship, we shout aloud in the din of a sinful world that our God is God and the sole remedy for a sinner's plight and position. In our praise and worship, we glorify our God and therefore light a saving candle that can be seen by those who are perishing in a dark and dying world of sin and lostness. Praise and worship is the interaction of every one of us with the other with the most divine Lord and God.

To answer the often asked question presented previously, "How are we as believers to serve and worship and praise such a God as this," we must explore our worship and praise. We must serve, worship and praise our Lord in the convergence of worship. This is the inter-weave of our service to our one Lord and God. The reader may cry foul and say I am being exclusive in this time of inclusiveness and he would be right. The reader may cry foul and say that I am being narrow in my understanding in this time of multiple paths to God and believe as you want as long as you believe in something or someone mentality so prevalent in today's world and he would be right. I do believe in an exclusive God and we must praise and worship Him exclusively. I believe that only He is the way, the truth and the light. I believe that only through Him can one find life in salvation from God's wrath against sin. I believe that He is a jealous God.

I believe in this time, one problem with the modern church is not the absence of programs and plans, but the presence of the world within the church. The exclusive light from an exclusive God via an exclusive praise and worship has been dimmed by the plans and programs of mankind utilizing the organizations and thought processes of the bottom line of the world. Perhaps the flock and lost are fleeing our churches because they no longer see the light from our candle. If the world is found in our churches and dimming the light of God, why bother to leave our houses. I believe in the convergence of worship and praise we shine the more brightly our candles of His saving light can be seen clearly in the storms of life by those who are drowning in the sway and tumult of the storm.

I have had the pleasure and joy of attending many and varied types of church services. Many have left me wanting in certain aspects without feeling complete within my spirit.

The Charismatic and Pentecostal churches left me with a feeling of *power* with their many signs glorifying God.

The evangelical churches gave me my *purpose* in service to the Lord; my mission to display God to the world. The sacramental services I have attended with its great liturgy and Mass gave me a peace with God in their *practice*. The silent prayer meetings of the Society of Friend's Church gave me this same peace.

The dispensational oriented churches gave me my *position* in the Lord. With their proclamation of this being the time of the age of grace and that we are members of the bride of the Lord through my salvation and justification by faith alone in the Lord's grace, I knew where I belonged in the Lord's scheme of things.

I believe that it is within these four streams of differing worship a believer is able to find true and complete worship and praise to our God. In the merging of our power, purpose, practice and position, we touch more completely our Lord. These types of worship and praise became to me a cycle depicting a completeness that is to be found in our convergence of worship.

The term 'convergence of worship' is not new to me. This term is used by the Charismatic Episcopal Church. This church denomination holds to a threefold convergence of the sacramental, evangelical and charismatic streams of worship while holding to a replacement theology akin to the Roman Catholic Church.[7]

I have added a fourth stream of convergence. This convergence is an additional element of the dispensational age of grace doctrine. I have removed further the point of view of the replacement theology not only held by the Charismatic Episcopal Church, but also by many mainline church denominations. I believe this doctrine and point of view violates Pauline writings (re. Romans chapters 9-11 to be the best example) concerning the role and position of the Jewish people and their future). I believe that we are in an interim between the 69th and the 70th week of Daniel in order to garner a bride for the Lord Jesus Christ.[8] I believe

---

[7] See, Non Nobis, Domine! The Convergence Movement and The International Communion of the Charismatic Episcopal Church by the Rev. Canon Philip E.P. Weeks with Mr. Hugh W. Kaiser, (c. Barnabas Ministries, Incorporate: Maitland, FL 32794) for a more complete rendering of their beliefs and practices.

[8] I have written previously in greater depth concerning this point of view within this work in the chapter Beginning Thoughts and in Book Two of "Concerning the Christ." FWB Publishing. c. 2011.

that to find complete worship and praise of our God we must reflect this doctrine of dispensationalism as our position along with the other three paths: our power, our purpose and our practice.

The Apostle John in the book of the Revelation of the Lord writes in chapter 4:6-9:

> **Before the throne there, was a sea of glass, like crystal. And in the midst of the throne, and around the throne, were <u>four living creatures</u> full of eyes in front and in back. The first living creature was <u>like a lion</u>, the second living creature <u>like a calf</u>, the third living creature had a face <u>like a man</u>, and the fourth living creature was <u>like a flying eagle</u>. The four living creatures, each having six wings, were full of eyes around and within. And <u>they do not rest day or night</u>, saying: Holy, holy, holy, Lord God Almighty, Who was and is and is to come!" Whenever <u>the living creatures give glory and honor and thanks to Him</u> who sits on the throne, who lives forever and ever, the twenty-four elders fall down before Him who sits on the   throne   and worship Him who lives forever and ever, and cast their crowns before the throne, saying: "You are worthy, O Lord, To receive   glory and honor and power; For You created all   things, And by Your will they exist and were created."**

He writes additionally of these four living creatures in chapter 5:6:

> **And I looked, and behold, in the midst of the throne and of the <u>four living creatures</u>, and in the**

midst of the elders, stood a Lamb as though it had been slain, having seven horns and seven eyes, which are the seven Spirits of God sent out into all the earth.

I think it not a coincidence that these four living creatures fly about God and declare God to be holy. I believe that in a symbolic manner they are a depiction of the cycle of complete praise and worship. Their function is to encircle the throne of God. In chapter 6 verse 2, with the Lamb (Jesus Christ) in their presence they give glory, honor, praise and reverence to the sovereign, holy, immutable, loving and infinite God in His heaven. God's throne in heaven is encircled by a convergence of worship and praise of the four living creatures. This worship and praise is followed by the twenty four elders (I believe to be the depiction of the church in heaven after the rapture). These living creatures, these special angels of holiness (they have six wings as do the seraphim angels) have four differing countenances in their worship of the Lord. Angels are messengers. As messengers they bear the messages of the one who has sent them. They bear the messages of God. They speak and cry out His messages. They can only speak of God. They declare His attributes and describe Him in His holiness. These four living creatures, these four angels continually cry and declare, "Holy, Holy, Holy." This declaration of God is continual and eternal. They declare His holiness and God is enthroned in their midst.

One is like a lion. This angel speaks of the _power_ of God. One is like a calf. This angel speaks of the _purpose_ of God. One is like a man. This speaks of a relationship or the _position_ of God. One is like an eagle. This angel speaks of the _practice_ and royal walk of God.

The Triune God has given power and gifts to His believers to glorify God in diverse signs and wonders. Paul writes that these gifts are present within the age of grace and therefore are found in today's dispensational economy. In the age in which we live as grace age believers. This is not meant to say that I believe as so many in modern Christianity that the Lord is akin to a type of spiritual ATM machine and we as believers can merely withdraw from God whatever we may desire. These gifts are meant to give power in order to glorify God and to show a lost world their need of a Savior. Our walk has never and will never be about the 'me', but it is always and totally about Him. Our power is not for us, but is always through and from and for and by and to Him. Our walk is about Him and will never be about us. Our gifts from God, our *charismata* in the Greek language must reflect this orientation of direction.

God has given to us our purpose in our Christian walk. We are His church. We are His hands and feet on this earth. Our purpose is to be evangelical in our witness. We are to share God the Son as our method of salvation and His plan to reconcile fallen mankind back unto Himself. His work is to be our work. The English word church is derived from the Greek word *kuriakos* which means: pertaining to the Lord. We are His church and we are to be His feet and hands. We are to walk His walk. We are to do His work.

God has given to His church a special position in this age of grace. He has charged God the Spirit to gather a bride for God the Son. We are to be a member of this bride. This position during this time is specific to the age of grace. Mankind has always lived in an economy (*oikonomia* in the Greek language from which we derive the word economy) or dispensation of the Lord's grace. Simply stated it means how we make our spiritual living during a particular time. During this time it is a dispensation of grace and the only method and manner by which we can be saved is through believing in His death, burial and resurrection and confessing this truth as our statement of faith. This position is a time of hiatus and an interim between the 69 weeks of Daniel and the 70th week which arises with the rapture of the bride and the onset of the Great Tribulation of the 70th week of Daniel.

God is not slack as we are. He has promised through His covenant promises certain promises to a certain people, the Jews and He will fulfill every promise He has made in His time.

God has given His practice to His believers to guide our walk. During our walk, He has given us His peace that we can reside in His presence. It is within His peace we can find our practice. No matter the situation. Whether sword or trials or pestilence or martyrdom we can know His peace. That is the peace that can pass any understanding. Those facing tribulation, facing the lions of the coliseum knew this peace. Those behind the iron curtain of atheistic communism knew this peace. In good times or in bad, we can know this peace. It must be our practice. The beauty of the Mass is that we can fill His peace in our liturgical rendering of His passion.

Within the cycle of the power, the purpose, the position and the practice we see the cycle of worship and praise. His charismata, His evangelical message, His dispensational promises and His peace are given to us to do His will. This cycle as are all cycles mentioned within this work is an interactive cycle.

A second cycle of praise and worship falls right in line with the first cycle mentioned above. We must reflect this holy God and glorify Him in our wonders, our work, our walk and our wait.

This cycle can be demonstrated by the seasons of the year: the spring; a time of newness, life and wonder in a powerful burst of activity and growth and demonstration, the summer; a time of work to spread the message of the gospel of the Lord in His grace, the autumn; a time of harvest, rest and peace which we can find in sacramental worship and praise and the winter; a time of stasis and interim awaiting the Spring.

The spring, I believe represents the charismatic aspect of praise and worship. The summer reflects the evangelical aspect. The autumn reflects the sacramental aspect. Lastly, I believe the winter reflects the dispensation aspect of worship and praise.

In all cycles and their symbolism, one can only maintain so much, but I have found these cycles of convergence to reflect the attributes of our mighty and sovereign God whom we serve. We know that these four living creatures continually declare the Lord to be holy and immutable and infinite and loving as do all creatures found in His presence. They declare His Lordship and that He is the creator God. I believe we must reflect the Lord in our service of praise and worship in charismatic power, evangelical purpose, sacramental practice and in our dispensational position. This convergence will allow and posit our praise and worship more completely as we serve the God of the universe. He deserves nothing less. As we present His gospel of the cross and resurrection, we can more brightly hold His candle as we display His light as believers of the true God to those who are in need.

Beginning Thoughts[9]

"The vague and tenuous hope that God is too kind to punish the ungodly has become a deadly opiate for the consciences of millions" *--A.W.Tozer*

This book deals with a particular concept in the reading Scripture. This concept is the utilizing of cyclical biblical interpretive models. By reading Scripture cyclically as opposed to lineally, the readers of the Bible can to a greater degree grasp and rightly divide the word of the Lord. With a greater understanding, our roles as believers in the grace of God will grow and we can be more and more like the Lord in our Christian walk. To paraphrase an axiom, "A text taken out of context is merely a pretext."

I have offered several examples within book two of utilizing cycles to rightly divide God's word. The examples are not exhaustive and I feel the whole of Scripture, from Genesis to Revelation is cyclical in nature.

Where to begin on such a challenging task? The Scripture for thousands of years has been interpreted and commented upon by many learned men and women. For too long, Scripture has been incorrectly used to substantiate a certain denomination or point of view. I believe this arises by not rightly dividing Scripture. Most folk reside in a particular denomination with a group in more or less agreement with each other. Each group will

---

[9] This chapter, Beginning Thoughts, was originally published in my book, *"Concerning the Christ,"* FWB Publishing. c. 2011.

argue they rightly exegete the word and their interpretation, coincidently agrees with their group or denomination. Does it? Do we read Scripture to prove we are right or do we read the Scripture to see and learn if we are wrong? If we are to be like the Bereans and be more excellent, we must read Scripture to ascertain if what we are taught and what we hear is correct. Perhaps we have been taught incorrectly. We must place aside our various and diverse traditions and see what Scripture says about a particular subject. The Bereans, found in the Acts of the Apostles were excellent because they looked in Scripture to see for themselves what was correct or just as important what was incorrect. The light of Scripture must be the beacon to illuminate our paths of Christian walk and not the point of view of commentators or speakers. The Bible is the last line of defense against error. We must lay aside our denominational bents and read Scripture afresh and with fear and trembling. We must ask ourselves if our particular opinion holds the proverbial water or are we just promoting a tradition of our elders, of our own fathers, like the Pharisees in the Lord's time.

To paraphrase the Apostle Paul, he considered himself to be all things to all men hoping to save some. He also warned us to seek out our own soul salvation in fear and trembling. Our search is somewhat like Carl Jung's concept of individuation in that we must discard the truths around and reach and obtain the truth that is for and before us as searchers. I hold and maintain the only truth one can reach in fruition and completeness is the truth of the Lord Jesus Christ. All other supposed truths at best are merely partial truths. Where to begin this task to grab onto the truth of the Lord? I offer this truth is found only in Christian scripture. This fact makes our rightly dividing His word of greater importance. Where to begin?

The first place of our search or any other is to have a starting place. We must have an intellectual and philosophical foundation from which to build our world view. We live in a day where too many folk wish to dumb down our existence and thoughts. We have become in our walk like an ostrich when confronted with a difficult situation sticks its head into the sand pretending the danger or difficulty is no longer there by merely being ignorant of its presence. I would offer that whether the ostrich can or cannot see anything matters little. The predator is still on the hunt. Truth is truth. We must be compelled, especially in the external realm to reach for the truth and not bury our heads in the sand. The predator of ignorance is about and will lead to our destruction.

This search for a philosophical and intellectual foundation should not scare us. Everyone in the world has a particular foundation from which he or she builds their world view. Simply put this foundation is what we believe to be true. What do you hold as true? This is the most basic definition of faith. What do you believe to be true? We structure and understand the world around us be the presence or absence of certain presuppositions. What a big word, but it only means what a person believes beforehand. What a person supposes beforehand. I am not using word, presupposition as in a certain denominational philosophical traditional manner. As an example, if I see a building, I can presuppose that it has structure and can support itself if I walk into it. Another example is if I see an automobile running down the road I can take for granted that it has some sort of engine propelling it. A last illustration is if I see a tree growing in a park, I can presuppose, accept that there are sufficient nutrients and water flowing through its root system to nourish the tree. The possession of presuppositions is by its definition essential to our understanding of our place in the universe.

I AM A CHRISTIAN

I am a Christian. The first place to begin the construction of our foundation is the presupposition, the taking as a fact that there is a God. We must start with the truth of the existence of God and secondly, we are not Him. These statements immediately place me into controversy. Most world views would disagree with the preceding three statements. In fact, I must say that in this day, the preceding three sentences would place me in controversy with many in Christianity.

The Gnostics with their numerous modern day variations would disagree with this point of view. The Christian Scientists, the adherents of Cabala and the devotees of New Ageism would disagree with me. These are but three examples of conflict. My first presupposition I am presenting is we are not gods, but there is a God.

I am only Christian. I do not believe in multiple paths to God. How can I? Our Lord was clear and succinct when in John's Gospel chapter 14:6 He declared that He was the way and the truth and the life and the only way to the Father was through Him. I can accept no other way. Any other way that is offered cannot in truth be reconciled to true Christianity regardless of what others within or without of Christianity may profess.

The God of our universe by definition is and must be the singularity of all things. There are those that cry out there is no God and dismiss this point of truth. They accept a world of meaning, but dismiss the existence of a meaningful order giver of that meaning. They boast their randomness, but cry foul if their rights and points of view are challenged. If life is random and darwinistic in its evolution, there is not one point of view better than another. There can only be what evolves into the next progeny that can be labeled a success. I do not believe in random chance. I believe there is a God and He is the creator God. He is the order giver of the universe. He is the meaning giver to the meaningful of this life. Most of the world is in disagreement with me. Let me narrow my scope a bit further and refine my thought.

CERTAIN ATTRIBUTES OF GOD

I believe in a Christian God. I do not believe in any other God save the Christian God. I believe this God is the creator and focus of all truth and reality in totality obtainable in this world. I believe via creation He is sovereign (He rules) and immutable (He never changes) and holy (He is divine and never sins) and loving and infinite (He forever was and will forever be).

He is sovereign in that He is the creator God and we are the created. This is just another way of saying that there is a God and we are not Him. He by virtue of His creatorship is omnipresent (everywhere), omniscient (all knowing), omnipowerful (all powerful). He is God and by His very definition He must be these things. He is God and He cannot help but be these things.

He is immutable and changes not. We live in world content with the intent of changing and repackaging everything with its grasp. 'A new coat of paint makes any old barn look better,' is their cry and slogan. Often they seem not to worry if the barn is structurally sound and worry only about its cosmetic look. This desire for the cosmetic and not about the structurally sound arises from our desire for the exotic. Our Lord must be immutable and unchangeable. If He was not, He is schizophrenic in His nature. In Scripture, He describes Himself as the alpha and omega (the first and last letters of the Greek alphabet, the 'a-z' utilizing our English alphabet, the beginning and the end. He is the everything and therefore unchangeable. He declares that He changes not.

He is holy in that He is spiritually pure. He is divine. By definition via His sovereignty, whoever He is and whatever He does must be holy. He is the definer of holiness. Also by definition via His holiness, anything removed and apart from Him must be unholy. We cannot pull the Lord down to our lever as many have done. We must reach up to Him and His level to find foundational truth.

He is loving in that He possesses the quality and quantity of emotion and compassion we describe as love. He cannot not love. He is love. He in particular loves human kind.

I believe He displays the attribute of infinitude meaning that He always has been God and will always be

God. As He was in the beginning, He is now and will be throughout future eternity.[10]

By defining the Lord as sovereign and immutable and holy and loving and infinite, I have organized and presupposed a world view that differs from the world and their constructions. If the Lord is as I have described, must of the world is wrong in their world view. I believe my position and world view is an absolutist position. Absolute is not a bad word. I believe this absolutely. In building our foundation and world view, we must understand a universe with a creator who is steady and always the same and constant and holy and loving and is forever and ever.

I believe this same God chose to deal with humanity in a particular way, a certain manner. In His way. In His manner. I cannot in my position as creation argue with Him over His method. I cannot beat my head against a proverbial brick way challenging His method. He is God and therefore my responsibility and duty is to conform to His plan. I cannot and choose not to anthropomorphize (changing into human form) God. Much of the world has chosen to do this changing of God. Others seek to form God into their image or desires or fantasies. I maintain a position that by doing this the world is not seeking God in truth. They are like the painters of that barn mentioned previously trying to repackage and remold God to fit their viewpoint and are merely slapping a new coat of paint of an exterior by their own vanity. They are not reaching for His truth. They are merely justifying themselves and their sin.

---

[10] The concept of the attributes of God; His infinitude, sovereignty, immutability, holiness and love among the many other attributes of God are best discovered in the many works and descriptions of A.W. Tozer. The Christian and Missionary Alliance pastor and writer.

By doing this repackaging, they are trying to relieve their guilt and remove any responsibility for their actions, wants and desires. Their barn from the outside is pretty, but the inside is only rotting wood. We ignorantly, like the before mentioned ostrich hide our heads hoping there is no predator. Vanity and ignorance are two voracious predators and will devour us as believers.

I believe the God of the universe chose not only to deal with humanity, but chose to reveal Himself in His own manner. He chose to come as a man, the Theoanthropic (the God-man).

I believe and presuppose that He chose to use certain human writers at different times through the auspices of God the Spirit to pen His canon to explain and illuminate Himself and His position. This does not mean God has exhaustively and completely revealed Himself in Scripture. It does mean that Scripture is complete and exhaustive in what is necessary for us to obtain reconciliation with God.

I hold, believe and presuppose this same God chose to reveal Himself in three Persons: God the Father, God the Son and God the Spirit. I believe in a Trinity. A Triunity. To paraphrase C. S. Lewis in his description of the Trinity found in "Mere Christianity:" God the Spirit is inside us as our teacher and unction, God the Son (Lord Jesus) is beside us interceding for us on our behalf, God the Father is before us and is our goal. Our understanding of this Trinity is only available in truth within Scripture and through the revelation of the Holy Spirit. I ardently believe that Scripture, the Word will always be in harmony with the Spirit. These two are given to us by God to anchor our tree of Christianity as two mighty roots to keep us from leaving the good anchor and being blown over with whatever wind of change that might happen our way. They will always be in harmony with the other.

Today we seem to have massive groups within Christianity who do not have harmony between the two. We have huge groups within the Christian community who rest upon some special revelation of a perceived spiritual source. From the existential to the pieties, the historic Christ and His Word has been regulated by some doctrine of man and now rests upon a coffee table gathering dust and not within our spirit, should, and mind. I believe John 1, the Word and John 14, the Spirit are for today and in harmony with the other. Without the two together, truth and true understanding cannot be realized.

CERTAIN COVENANTS

I believe God chose to deal with a certain group of humanity through a series of covenant promises. This method is His right, for He is God and sovereign. Covenants or contracts; to Adam (both in the Garden of Eden and after the fall of Adam and Eve), to Seth, to Noah, to Abraham and his offspring and furthered modified with Moses (the Law), David (an eternal throne) and about Palestine (a specific geography) were given and have been or will be fulfilled. The covenants made and secured by God are detailed in the prophecies made to and through the covenant people.

The 70 weeks prophecy as outlined in Daniel 9 specifically deal with the fulfillment of the covenants by the Messiah and His kingdom and His kingdom people, His covenant people, the Jew. From Genesis 1 through Acts 7 we see the development of the progressively revealed covenants. From Genesis 12 (Abraham) through Acts 7 (martyrdom of Stephen and his declaration of the Messiahship of Jesus Christ and the rejection of this declaration by the Jews who martyred him) we see God dealing specifically with a particular people, the Jews. I am always surprised by the reactions of people of this fact. Understanding Scripture must be seen in the light of this development.

With their rejection of the Jewish Messiah, the Lord Jesus Christ, we see that these promises have been put on hold for an indeterminate time. The Lord beginning with Acts 8 began to deal with all of humanity again with the calling of Paul and the gospel of grace. I believe that we dwell in the age of grace. An age not to fulfill covenant promises, but to garnet from this age of the gentiles a bride for the Groom. The bride is the church. The Groom is the Lord Jesus Christ. Grace promises are offered to all of humanity and not only for the covenant people, the Jews, re. Romans chapters 9-11. To be a believer in this age of grace one must believe in their heart and confess with their mouth the death, burial and resurrection of Jesus Christi. I find not where in Scripture outside of Paul's letters and the Letter to the Hebrews where this is the method of salvation. The purpose of the age of grace is not to usher in the kingdom of the Messiah as is the case of Genesis 12 through Acts 7. The purpose of grace is to gather a bride for the Groom.

With the gathering of the gentiles (including all Jews who believe and confess the death, burial and resurrection of Lord Jesus, the church will be called away in a rapture, *harpasdo* in the Greek. Many may cry foul that this concept of a snatching away is found only within Pauline writings. I agree with these folk. It is a dispensational truth about this dispensation, *oikonomia*, of grace. The word, *oikonomia* is the origin of our English word, economy. The dispensation of grace means simply how one makes his spiritual living in this particular time. In this age of grace, we must believe in our hearts and confess with our mouths the death, burial and resurrection of the Lord, Romans 10:9-13 and 1 Corinthians 15:1-4. When the fullness of the times of the gentiles is achieved, the bride of Christ will be summoned away in the rapture.

This is not a contradiction of scripture from Genesis 1 through the calling out of Paul. The covenants of the true God will be completed, but due to the rejection of the Jews a hiatus has been placed on prophecy to fulfill this grace economy.

With the rapture accomplished, the covenant timetable and promises with be finished and accomplished with the ushering in of the 70th week of Daniel. We more popularly refer to this 70th week as the Tribulation and it was prophesied by Jesus Christ and penned by John the Revelator.

I do not believe God's program with the Jewish people is over or assumed by the Christian church. Every promise God made to Israel will be fulfilled by this same sovereign, immutable, holy, love, and infinite God. I believe that Origen and Augustine and many others, through true to the Lord and profound in their writings were wrong in their understanding of the biblical concept that the church has replaced the Jews. I believe that many church denominations though sincere in their holding to this replacement theology are sincerely wrong and have misinterpreted Scripture concerning this issue.

Some reader may wish to cry that I am presenting a gospel that is a hodgepodge or an olio, but I disagree. The covenant or contract made to Adam by God in the Garden of Eden was not rescinded by the Fall, but with the failure of man to be true to God's contract it was altered with a further revealed covenant.

Genesis 3 was not voided by the covenant given by the birth of Seth, a messianic line and man started to call on the name of God instead of the reverse. The Edenic and Adamic Covenant remain in effect, but God's plan has been more progressively revealed with the Sethic Covenant, Genesis 4:25-26.

Humankind did not remain true to this covenant as with the others and broke it. Therefore God brought about the Noahic Covenant. The promises made to Noah; the eating of meat and the existence of governmental authority, i.e. capital punishment for murder did not do away with the Edenic, Adamic, or the Sethic Contracts.

The Noahic Covenant again was the further progressed revealed will of God. This has been true throughout the covenant times. From Genesis 1 through Acts 7, God has made contracts with specific people concerning specific promises. In these cases, man has failed to live up to their part of the bargain and therefore the contract has been rescinded. With the contract voided due to man's failure, God is free to rewrite or enlarge the parameters of the contract which He has done.

The Noahic Covenant was broken by man and God called out a specific man, Abram and made a specific contract with him and his descendants, the Jews, Genesis 12-15. God promised Abram (Abraham) a land, a people, and a kingdom. These promises remain the cornerstone of the covenants and prophecy from Genesis 12 through Acts 7.

There have been additional refinements made by God to the Abrahamic Covenant. The Law given to Moses, Exodus and the promises made by God to King David and his everlasting throne and kingdom, Psalm 132:11-13 are two examples of these further progressions made by God.

Entire books and lessons are given concerning these covenant promises made by God. All of these promises will be fulfilled by God through the Messiahship of God the Son, the Lord Jesus Christ. I believe this plan of God is consistent with all prophecy. Psalm2, Psalm 22, Psalm 110 and Daniel 9 (the 70th week prophecy) are just a few examples.

In Acts 7 with the rejection of the Jews concerning the Messiahship of the Lord and the martyrdom of Stephen, the Lord in His providence has put a pause on these covenant promises for an indeterminate time. He has chosen in His sovereignty to deal with the entire world with the gospel of grace. In this time of His grace, we are saved not to be part of His kingdom, though we will be, but to be His bride. His promises to us are not earthly as were the promises made to Adam, Seth, Noah, Abraham, Isaac, Jacob, their descendants, Moses and David, but they are heavenly, the Epistle to the Colossians chapter 1:3. I believe this method of the Lord is consistent with His nature as Elohim Olam, where we translate variously as the everlasting God, the God of time and the God of secrets. I believe due the failure of the Jews to accept the Messiahship of the Lord, the God of time chose to call out a group from the gentiles to garner a bride. A bride we call the church. This is not inconsistency on God's part, but the plan of God. In His omniscience, there came a time for another dispensation or administration of God to be revealed. I believe this is the time of the age of grace. These are the mysteries which were revealed to the Apostle Paul. If these mysteries were revealed to Paul then they were secret before Paul and God's revelation to him. This is the church age, the age of the bride. This is our time. An interval has occurred. This is not a prophetic time as is the covenant promises, but a time for the Holy Spirit to be like the unnamed servant of Abraham to acquire a bride for the father's son. God the Spirit is to collect a bride for the Son of God the Father who is God the Son, the Lord Jesus Christ.

Let me restate; the covenant promises are concerning the Messiahship of the Lord Jesus Christ and the institution of His kingdom. The grace promises found in the Pauline writings are concerning the time of the gentiles and the gathering of a chaste bride for the Son of God. This time is not a contradiction, but a hiatus, an interval. The goal of the covenants is to fulfill the promises God made specifically to specific people. The goal of the grace age is to gather a bride. They are different goals and orientations, but both within the plan and providence of the Lord. Both fulfill the plan a demonstrated and spoke of throughout Scripture. Both point to the singular point of grace who is our Lord and Savior Jesus Christ.

This focus of God upon the fallen lot of humankind is the crux of which the entire history of time and mortality revolve. This focus of God and His plan to redeem a sinful disobedient group back to Himself through Himself is the point of time that everything before must be viewed and the light of and by which everything after must be explained.

The Apostle Paul was called by this same Jesus Christ on the Damascus Road specifically to carry this gospel of grace to the entire world. He came speaking and saying that he knew nothing but Christ and Christ crucified. I believe in our time this must be our message. This is the true message. The death, burial and resurrection of the Lord in this age is the defining moment of grace. It must transcend everything and define all. Our church must be seen in the light of this gospel. Our history, doctrines, world views, and everything rest upon this message.

I am dispensational. This is another presupposition which I believe. All things must be seen through the lens of the finished work of the cross. No complete or true understanding can be had without the awareness and belief of this great moment of interaction and intervention between God and mankind. Many of the problems within the Christian community arise when we desire to add something to this gospel. The gospel of the Christ must stand alone. It is the start of the journey for all truth, faith, and belief, Hebrews 11:1, 6. With this death, burial, and resurrection via belief and confession of the same, we have started to grow our tree of salvation graciously given from God to once fallen mankind. From that tree, we can hang our fruits and works and activities in our imitation of Him, 1 Corinthians 11:1 and Ephesians 5:1.

A CYCLICAL APPROACH

Another presupposition I believe is the world is cyclical in nature. I believe the understanding of scripture must be achieved by understanding that Scripture is written cyclically. Through the utilization of what I have termed cyclical biblical interpretive models, a reader can more fully grasp what our Lord is saying to us in His word, the Bible.

All of nature demonstrates cycles. All of life reflects cycles. One example is the cycle of the year. It is not circular, but is cyclical. A year begins and revolves and closes and then begins anew. Points of view other than this cyclical pattern become just points of myopia, near-sightedness. We have missed the year and have seen only a day of the year. We missed the big picture and have become bogged down with the minutiae. Being myopic, one can only reflect points and not the cycle and therefore cannot reflect the totality of His truth.

In my youth, there was a cartoon figure, Mr. Magoo. He suffered from myopia. He would live his cartoon life and functioned, but he suffered from confusion and mistakes arising from his near-sightedness. Of course these occurrences to him were not confusing or mistakes. He perceived his reality to be real. He would argue with coat racks upon which hung a hat and an umbrella, but to Mr. Magoo was a person who was snubbing him. It was wonderful fun to watch Mr. Magoo walk through his cartoon existence with his missteps and mistakes. Most of us in defining truth live our lives like Mr. Magoo. We perceive through spiritual and intellectual eyes with a form of myopia. This prevents us from seeing clearly. This is true when we read Scripture. Many of us read Scripture with the myopic eyes of a certain denominational slant or a philosophical school of thought.

The absence of cyclical interpretive models is a myopic rendering of exegesis. Without the cycle, we see only points on the cycle. We grab a verse here or snatch a portion of Scripture there and we have missed the meaning of the text. We have taken a text out of context which leaves us only a pretext. Most of the conflicts and seeming contradictions within the Christian community arise from this absence of context. Calvinism and Wesleyanism are not contradictory. Both are two points on the cycle of the interaction of God's sufficient grace and man's free will. One side, Calvinism veers to the side of the sufficiency of grace whereas Wesleyanism veers toward man's given free will. In the context of salvation, we are saved through the given grace of the Lord and our accepting this grace as free moral agents. This is but one example.

Most doctrinal denominational beliefs stem from a rendering of Scripture through myopic eyes. We then build a building and create a denomination to encapsulate our doctrine. Within the confines of our edifices, we encourage and lead others into conversion. We train devotees and converts of our churches into becoming reflections of our myopia. Instead of imitating the Lord and His death, burial, and resurrection, we make Christians who reflect our denominations. They are saved through the blood of the Lord and His passion and resurrection, but myopic in their understanding. Many never are able to grasp the totality of truth that has been given to us in Scripture and taught to us by the Holy Spirit. I believe that a complete understanding of Scripture is obtainable through understanding and utilizing cycle biblical interpretive models.

THE HIGH HOLY DAYS

Another cycle demonstrated within Scripture is the yearly calendar of the Jewish High Holy Feast Days. This yearly calendar reflects the prophetic calendar of our Lord and includes the interims of the church age and the millennial kingdom of the returned Messiah.

When first given by the Lord, the beginning of the Jewish calendar began in the spring of the year. The High Holy Days reflect this time table. In the spring of the year, the first feast day is Passover until the last feast which is the Feast of Dedication (Chanukah though not one of the seven High Feast days is cited in Scripture and was celebrated by the Lord and is included in this cycle) we can see the fulfillment of all things. The High Holy Feasts of Israel are typologies and shadows of what we and will be completed through the Messiah, the Lord Jesus Christ.

The first feast, Passover was a type and demonstrated the death and shed blood of our Lord. Through the shedding of blood, the death angel knew to pass over the Jews in the Egyptian captivity. In like manner, through the shed blood of our Savior, we have our sins forgiven and we have the wrath of God against sin pass over us as believers.

The second feast is the Feast of Unleavened Bread and demonstrated His burial in holiness. He is without sin and is apart from the worldliness of the fallen world. He is separated.

The third feast is the Feast of Firstfruits and is a wave offering of the first harvest feast day. In like kind, our Lord is the Firstfruits in His resurrection. His resurrection is the power of our salvation, Romans 1:17 and 18. He was not resuscitated, but He is the resurrection and the life.

The fourth feast is the Feast of Pentecost which was the second harvest feast day. Pentecost was fulfilled with the coming of the second comforter, *parakletos* in the Greek, the Holy Spirit promised by the first comforter, Jesus Christ in the Gospel of John 14. With the second comforter given to the Jewish people present in Jerusalem, some three thousand souls accepted the Messiahship of the Lord.

There is an interim between the first four feasts and the next three. I believe this interim to be the current age of grace.

With the completion of this interim Rosh Hashanah, the Feast of Trumpets comes in the fall of the year. I believe this feast serves two purposes; the first concerning the church and the second concerning the covenant promises made throughout Scripture. Concerning the church, Rosh Hashanah demonstrates the rapture or catching away of the bride, the church. The bride is to be stolen away from this fallen land by the Groom, the Lord and taken to His Father's house.

Rosh Hashanah, concerning the covenants, shadows the calling back of Israel for a season of repentance and prophetically demonstrates the return of the covenant economy and the beginning of the 70th week of Daniel.

This time is symbolized by the feast, Yom Kippur, the Feast of Atonement and is a season of confession. This time is what we call the Tribulation. This time centers upon Israel primarily, but of course is worldwide in scope. The 70th week prophecy of Daniel is fully demonstrated by Yom

Kippur and this great Tribulation ends with the second coming of the Messiah.

This second coming is represented by the Feast of Tabernacles and will be the institution of the Lord's kingdom.

There is another interval between the Feast of the Tabernacles and Chanukah. I believe this interval to be the time of the kingdom. The duration of the kingdom period on earth is one thousand years and in its turn will be completed with the final judgment over sin and evil, the Great White Throne Judgment.

Chanukah, the Feast of Dedication is an eighth feast symbolizing a new beginning and is symbolic of the beginning of eternity for all the believers of the various economies, dispensations of the Lord. Chanukah commemorates the rededication of the Temple during the Maccabean Revolt and will be spiritually fulfilled with the restoration of the new Heaven and new Earth and the coming of the New Jerusalem.

This cycle of the High Holy Days is symbolic of the cycle of restoration and gives completion for all the prophecy and grace given so graciously by the Lord Jesus the Christ, Yeshua the Messiah. All of creation will find its restoration and completion in the Lord.

In conclusion, I believe in a Christian God who intervenes within the world's history and has made provision for our lost predicament. I believe He has revealed Himself in history personally to us in the presence and life, death, burial, and resurrection of Jesus Christ, God the Son. I believe He talks to us today through Scripture,

His word and the Spirit, God the Spirit. I believe that at all times the Spirit and the Scripture will be harmonious with each other. If your revelation is not harmonious with Scripture then something is wrong with your revelation. I believe the plan of God has been dispensationally and progressively revealed throughout history. I believe we not live in a dispensation, economy of grace. This interval was given due the rejection of the Messiah in order to gather a bride for the Groom. I believe that Scripture is best understood utilizing the cycles present within Scripture. These are some of my basic presuppositions when I read the word of God.

SALVATION[11]

YOU LOVE BROKE THROUGH
Like a foolish dreamer
Trying to build a highway to the sky
All my hopes would come tumbling down
And I never knew just why
Until today when You pulled away the clouds
That hung like curtains on my eyes
Well I've been blind, all these wasted years
And I thought I was so wise
But then You took me by surprise
All my life I've been searching
For that crazy missing part
And with one touch You just rolled away
The stone that held my heart
And now I see that the answer
Was as easy as just asking You in
And I am so sure I could never doubt
Your gentle touch again
It's like the power of the wind
Like waking up from the longest dream
How real it seemed.
Until Your love broke though
I've been lost in a fantasy
That blinded me.
Until Your love broke through[12]
-Keith Green, Todd Fishkind, Randy Stonehill

---

[11] This chapter, "Salvation," was originally titled, "The Table of Salvation," was originally found in my work, "Concerning the Christ," FWB Publishing. C. 2011.
[12] Keith Green, Todd Fishkind, Randy Stonehill, "Your Love Broke Through," copyright, 1976, 1977 April Music, Inc./King of Hearts Publishing (ASCAP).

PSALMS 51

Have mercy upon me, O God, according to Your loving kindness; according to the multitude of Your tender mercies, blot out my transgressions.

Wash me thoroughly from my iniquity, and cleanse me from my sin.

For I acknowledge my transgressions, and my sin is always before me.

Against You, You only, have I sinned, and done this evil in Your sight – that You may be found just, when You speak, and blameless when You judge.

Behold, I was brought forth in iniquity, and in sin my mother conceived me.

Behold, You desire truth in the inward parts, and in the hidden part You will make me to know wisdom.

Purge me with Hyssop, and I shall be clean; wash me, and I shall be whiter than snow.

Make me hear joy and gladness, that the bones You have broken may rejoice.

Hide Your face from my sins, and blot out all my iniquities.

Create in me a clean heart, O God, and renew a steadfast spirit within me,

Do not cast me away from Your presence, and do not take Your Holy Spirit from me,

Restore to me the joy of Your salvation, and uphold me by Your generous Spirit.

Then I will teach transgressors Your ways, and sinners shall be converted to You.

Deliver me from the guilt of bloodshed, O God, the God of my salvation, and my tongue shall sing aloud of Your righteousness.

O Lord, open my lips, and my mouth shall show forth Your praise.

For You do not desire sacrifice, or else I would give it; You do not delight in burnt offering.
The sacrifices of God are a broken spirit, a broken and a contrite heart – these, O God, You   will not despise.
Do good in Your good pleasure to Zion; build the walls of Jerusalem.
Then You shall be pleased with the sacrifices of righteousness, with burnt offering and whole   burnt offering; then they shall offer bulls on Your altar.

King David of ancient Israel found himself in a predicament, a quandary. He had a problem. His problem is akin to our problem. Sin. None of us can hide from our sin. In the final analysis, we all must hear our own Nathan stand before us displaying our vanity and pride and hear him say what we already knew, "Thou are the man," 2 Samuel 12:7. With King David his sin was murder and adultery; the murder of Uriah the Hittite and the adultery with Uriah's wife, Bathsheba.

We all are that 'man'. I am that 'man'. We are sinful and lost. We all require a remedy. We all are in need of a Savior. To paraphrase the Apostle Paul in his letter to the Romans, we are without excuse. God in His sovereignty, love, mercy, holiness and infinitude deemed to provide those lost and dying a gift, His grace. The Lord Jesus Christ, God the Son is that grace. Grace, *charis* in the Greek, means gift. We could not buy our salvation. It had to be given to us.

The table of salvation is the altar of God and is found in the interaction between God's sufficient grace and our given free will. I consider our salvation experience to be like a table in which God brings His grace, the given sacrifice and passion of God the Son, the Lord Jesus Christ; His death, burial and resurrection (I Corinthians 15:1-4) and our faith, *pistis* in the Greek or what we hold to be true. A.W. Tozer writes, "What I believe about God is the most important thing about me."

Faith is not the dismissal of rationale as the modern secularist, existentialist or even the pietist suggests, but the acceptance as true the reason of God, both natural and revealed. To state it in simple terms, "Did God do what He said He did?" Faith is the affirmation as fact concerning the gift, the Lord Jesus Christ and His grace. It is in the interaction of God's grace and our free will at this table of salvation where the remedy of man's lostness and sin can be found.

God's grace is sufficient. In the letter to the Hebrews 1:1-4 the scribe writes of who this gift is:

> **God, who at various times and in various ways spoke in time past to the fathers by the, has in these last days spoken to us by His Son, whom He has appointed heir of all things, through whom also He made the worlds, who being the brightness of His glory and the express image of His person and upholding all things by the word of His power, when He had by Himself purged our sins, sat down at the right hand of the Majesty on high, having become so much better than the angels, as He has by inheritance obtained a more excellent name than they.**

From all eternity past, God the Son, the Lord Jesus Christ was and is and will be the instrument in this plan of salvation.

In John's Gospel 1:1-5, we read:

In the beginning was the Word, and the Word was with God, and the Word was God. He was in the beginning with God. All things were made through Him, and without Him nothing was made that was made. In Him was life, and the life was the light of men. And the light shines in the darkness, and the darkness did not comprehend it.

God the Son is the Word of God. The *logos* in the Greek, the communication of God. *Logos* is the noun form of *lego*, to speak. He talks to us through His Word, the Scripture. Our Savior is the communicator God. *Logos* is also the root for the English word logical and therefore reasonable. Whatever our God speaks is not irrational and without reason. Our inability to comprehend does not indicate a weakness or shortcoming of His Word, but only our inability to comprehend.

In Paul's letter to the church at Colosse 1:13-20 we find:

He has delivered us from the power of darkness and conveyed us into the kingdom of the Son of His love, in whom we have redemption through His blood, the forgiveness of sins. He is the image of the invisible God, the firstborn over all creation. For by Him all things were created that are in heaven and that are on earth, visible and invisible,

whether thrones or dominions or principalities or powers. All things were created through Him and for Him. And He is before all things, and in Him all things consist. And He is the head of the body, the church, who   is the beginning, the firstborn from the dead, that in all things He may have the preeminence. For it pleased the Father that in Him all the fullness should dwell and by Him to reconcile all things to Himself, by Him, whether things on   earth or things in heaven, having made peace through the blood of His cross.

The Apostle Paul continues in this letter chapter 2:8-17:

Beware lest anyone cheat you through philosophy and empty deceit, according to the tradition of men, according to the basic principles of the world, and not according to Christ. For in Him dwells all the fullness of the Godhead bodily; and you are complete in Him, who is the head of all principality and power. In Him you were also circumcised with the circumcision made without hands, by putting off the body of the sins of the flesh, by the circumcision of Christ, buried with Him in baptism, in which you also were raised with Him through faith in the working of God, who raised Him from the dead. And you being dead in your trespasses and the un-circumcision of your flesh, He has made alive together with Him, having forgiven you all trespasses, having wiped out the handwriting of requirements that was against us, which was contrary to us. And He has taken it out of the way, having nailed it to the cross. Having disarmed principalities and powers, He made a public

spectacle of them, triumphing over them in it. So let no one judge you in food or in drink, or regarding a festival or a new moon or Sabbaths, which are a shadow of things to come, but the substance is of Christ.

Jesus the Christ is the head of the body and our creator God. We have our salvation and redemption through His forgiveness by His passion and resurrection. Our salvation is complete in Him.

Jesus the Christ was and is and will always be God. He is the Savior and the instrument of the plan to reconcile mankind back to Himself. He is the communicator of God. When we read Scripture we are reading His words. God the Spirit will never speak what is contrary to what is written in the Word. Of these preceding facts, we can rest and rely. We must hold onto these facts and believe them to be true.

HIS SAVING PURPOSE

This interaction of a sovereign, loving, immutable, holy and infinite God occurs in order to reconcile and lost mankind back to Himself and is the purpose of God. God has many purposes, but in regards to ourselves and our salvation this is a primary purpose. Mankind, through his free will had fallen via the disobedience of Adam. This act doomed all of us to be lost, but God in his mercy and grace had other plans. Through the passion and resurrection of Jesus Christ, our sins have been paid for. The judgment has been satisfied by God Himself and we can grab hold onto God's salvation. A.W. Tozer writes:

When God would make his name known to mankind He could find no better Word than. "I Am, I Am that I Am," says God. "I change not." Everyone and everything else measures from that fixed point.

YHWH, Jehovah, from the Hebrew verb root, *to be, I AM*. My, oh my what a God! He was and is and will be. His very name shows His sovereignty and unchangeableness and holiness and love and infinitude. These five and every other characteristic of which A.W. Tozer writes within his various works are found in the very name God chose to reveal to Moses.

HIS SPIRITUAL PREDICATE

A predicate or a verb denotes an action or a state of being. What does one mean when we speak of God's spiritual predicate? What is the motivation for His plan? What is the underlying reason for the plan of God? The Apostle Paul writes of God's motivation in Romans 5:8:

But God demonstrates His own love toward us, in that while we were still sinners, Christ died for us.

His predicate is love. It always has been so. Our God did not want mankind to reside without a resolution for his lost state. His plan for man's path of reconciliation back to Himself was, is and always will be His love. His grace is a gift of love. God through His love has paid the price for many even before we were here to accept or reject the gift.

HIS SUPREME PLAN

God has a purpose; to reconcile lost mankind back to Himself. We have discussed this previously. God has a predicate for that purpose; His love directed toward us. Thirdly, God has a plan. His plan of salvation is based and driven on two imperatives or absolutes. The first is that the penalty of sin can only be paid via the instrument of the shedding of blood. This absolute is stated first in Genesis 3 with the Lord shedding animal's blood to clothe Adam and Eve. This clothing was necessary so they would not be bare in the presence of a holy God. The writer of Hebrews in chapter 9:22 continues this biblical theme:

There is no remission . . .
without the shedding of the blood

This absolute of the creator is why Christ had to shed His blood on the cross of Golgotha. The debt could only be paid by the divine. The debt had to be paid and the Lord paid the price. This death and the shedding of divine blood followed by His burial and His resurrection is the noblest definition of redemption any can illustrate. This is the determinate for the grace of God. God the Son paid the penalty due us.

The second absolute or imperative of God is we in order to be considered just must live by faith. We must live and be sustained by what we believe to be true. We must believe and confess the death, burial and resurrection of the Lord in order to be considered just. One example is found in Hebrews 10:38:

The just shall live by faith . . .

We read of this requirement all throughout Scripture. Habakkuk 2:4 is another clear example. All who would be considered just by a just God must, "**believe that God is and that He is a rewarder of those who diligently seek Him,**" Hebrews 11:6.

Faith and belief, *pisits* and *pisteuo* in the Greek, or what we trust as true must be the finished work of the cross of the Lord. We must live and abide in His truth.

The previous two imperatives are driven by His spiritual predicate. Love describes God's motivation and the sufficient and all caring grace offered in conjunction with man's belief/faith/truth found at the table of salvation. We find this intersection in the gospel of the Lord, 1 Corinthians 15:1-4 cited throughout this text.

SERVANT'S SONG

I heard the trembling voice
Of one who did His will
Tears from eyes and heart
A voice shaking and so still
I don't think she noticed
Her solo was not at all
I heard her mom also singing
From a distant majestic hall
Christ compelled both to go
When they would rather stay
Both singing so far apart
Compelled me to pray
I cannot sing as they
But in a future day or night
I will sing a song with both
Of my Lord's mercy and might
I don't think it possible
To voice a complete thank you
For His song and that vision
And the hope He gave me too
Being promised life eternal
Someday He, I will see
One reason, that visional song
Her mom and she sang to me

-David E. Clarke, 10-91

THE GOSPEL

There has arisen in our modern age various and diverse gospels. The English word gospel comes from the Old English, 'God spell' and means good news, *euangellion* in the Greek, a message. In this age of diversity and differing messages, what is the Christian message? Many offer this or that in various and differing complexities and understandings of what is the gospel. What we need to offer the world may seem an arduous chore for us to undertake. The Christian message has been fractured in the Christian community. With the danger of being labeled an anachronism, I have retreated to our last line of defense for truth. I have gone to Scripture to present a pure and unadulterated gospel. I believe this simple message is the biblical message. It is the gospel presented by the Apostle Paul, the apostle called by the Lord to take the message of grace to the gentiles. It is found throughout the Pauline letters, but is found in its greatest clarity and succinctness in Paul's letter 1 Corinthians 15:1-4:

> **Moreover, brethren, I declare to you the gospel which I preached to you, which also you received and in which you stand, by which also you are saved, if you hold fast that word which I preached to you – unless you believed in vain. For I delivered to you first of all that which I also received: that Christ died for our sins according to the Scriptures, and that He was   buried, and that He rose again that third day according to the Scriptures. . .**

This is the gospel which Paul declared and preached. It is the gospel that the Corinthians received and stood upon. It is the gospel by which they were saved. The Apostle Paul states clearly that this is the gospel which he received. This begs the question, by whom did he receive this gospel? The answer is that he received this gospel to take to the gentiles from the risen Lord Jesus Christ. It is the gospel for this age of grace in the dispensation that we now find ourselves.

I find it significant this portion of Scripture is found right after chapters 12 through 14 of 1 Corinthians. Chapter 12 deals with various gifts of the Spirit. Chapter 13 deals with the preeminence of love. Chapter 14 readdresses the gifts received from the Spirit. Paraphrasing the Apostle Paul, "In addition to what I have just said, fellow believers I declare to you the message that I preached to you and you received as a sermon and by which you stand your ground in your mortal walk of belief and how you became believers and were saved by this truth . . . For I preached this message to you what I received myself from the Lord and this is the gospel message of the cross; the death, burial and resurrection of God the Son." He follows this gospel rendition, this message, *euaggelion*, with a list of eyewitnesses to the resurrection which would be compelling in any court room, i.e., Simon Greenleaf, John Warrick Montgomery and Philip Johnson's works concerning this issue. Between the gifts of the Spirit and the witnesses of the resurrection rest the gospel of the Lord.

The writer of Hebrews adds to this thought in chapter 13:20-21:

Now may the God of peace who brought up our Lord Jesus from the dead, that great Shepherd of the sheep, through the blood of the everlasting

covenant, make you complete in every good work to do His will, working in you what is well pleasing in His sight, through Jesus Christ, to whom be glory forever and ever. Amen.

Notice the resurrection; **brought up our Lord Jesus from the dead**, the shedding of the blood, **through the blood of the everlasting covenant** and the efficacy, the effectiveness of this grace, **make you complete in every good work to do His will**.

When a believer believes this gospel message, he will have the proverbial blinders removed from his eyes. He will see the grace of God is found everywhere in Scripture. In this age of grace, God's grace is found in the death and burial and resurrection of God the Son. Those blinders removed from the believer will allow the believer to read Scripture from cover to cover, verse upon subsequent verse, book after book and see the truth of God; understanding more completely the message of the Lord. That God loved us and would not leave us without provision from our sin and disobedience. He made a plan to reconcile fallen man back to Himself through Himself and by Himself. A text out of context leaves the reader only a pretext. Our understanding of what the gospel message is for this age will help us avoid any pretext.

We see the working of the spiritual predicate of God with the two spiritual imperatives in Genesis 3 with God's gift of clothing Adam and Eve with a type of spiritual clothing and Adam's act of faith and belief in naming the woman Eve, the mother of all living. Adam believed and trusted in the Lord's shedding of the animal's blood to allow mankind's communion with God to continue.

We see this grace/faith principle with Noah in Genesis 9. God's grace is found in saving Noah and his family in an ark of refuge and safety. The ark pitched and waterproofed with pitch, *kafar* in the Hebrew. This word for pitch is the same word also translated as atonement. Noah's faith in believing God to be true and entering the ark along with God closing the door allowed Noah and his family to rise above the torrential flood of God's judgment and wrath against the sins of the world. They were saved by Noah's faith in the grace of God.

We see this interaction of grace and faith with Abraham in Genesis 12 and 15. God called Abraham from Ur and Abraham has left his family to journey to a new land. In the chapters mentioned above, God promised him a land, a people and a government. Abraham believed these promises and via this belief, righteousness is imputed to Abraham, Romans 4.

Blinders have fallen from our eyes and the reality of the gospel of the Lord is beginning to fill our vision. All through Scripture it is the Lord and His promises that are displayed and demonstrated. We find all through Scripture this grace/faith principle. God gives to His chosen people and we must believe what He has given to be true. This must be our foundation, our reality upon which we stand, Hebrews 11:1.

Throughout Scripture we see shadows of the grace which finds its fruition in the cross, the death and the burial and resurrection of the Lord. The finished work at Calvary is the greatest event of all time. We find God doing such a wondrous thing for a disobedient group who deserved judgment, but received grace and mercy.

We are not only recipients of and respondents to this grace, but we become ministers of this plan of reconciliation by God. We read in 1 Corinthians 5:17-21:

> **Therefore, if anyone is in Christ, he is a new creation; old things have passed away; behold, all things have become new. Now all things are of God, who has reconciled us to Himself through Jesus Christ, and has given us the ministry of reconciliation, that is, that God was in Christ reconciling the world to Himself, not imputing their trespasses to them, and has committed to us the word of reconciliation. Now then, we are ambassadors for Christ, as though God were leading through us: we implore you on Christ's behalf, be reconciled to God. For He made Him who knew no sin to be sin for us, that we might become the righteousness of God in Him.**

Our purpose, our ministry is to be the feet and hands of the Lord and exhort and offer to a lost and dying world the Lord's plan for their salvation. Our purpose is the asking of the age old question, "What will you do with this Christ?' "What say you to Christ?" This is our banner we wave. This is our message we proclaim and preach. This is our gospel. We now find the interweave of all Scripture. It is the message Paul proclaims in 1 Corinthians 1:23, **". . . but we preach Christ crucified . . ."** Additionally he writes in chapter 2:2, **"For I determined not to know anything among you except Jesus Christ and Him crucified."**

In conclusion, with the Lord's sufficient grace and our interacting free will and having the finished work of the cross as our lifeline and beacon we sit at His table of salvation. We clearly can see the reality of what the Lord has done for us. Seeing His grace more clearly and with the guiding inspiration of the Holy Spirit, we can read what the Spirit has inspired, the words of God the Son through mortal writers. Read now Paul's Letter to the Romans and glean a portion of what we receive at the Lord's Table of salvation. We receive salvation from God's wrath against sin of course, but additionally we achieve: justification, redemption, the Holy Spirit, power, propitiation, perseverance, the gospel, belief in the Lord, character, righteousness, peace, God's demonstrative love, grace, the new man, the 2nd/ new Adam, hope of the Lord, new life, the baptism in the death and burial and resurrection of the Lord, glory in the Lord, glory in this life, the law of the Spirit, adoption, we become a slave of righteousness, eternal life, freedom from legalism/law of the body/the law of the mind, freedom from indwelling sin, God's foreknowledge, the conforming into the image of the son, freedom from condemnation. Oh my, what a Lord we serve and what a table He has given us to sit. We are complete in Him and His table is sufficient and ample for our situation or condition.

C.S. Lewis in his great work, "Mere Christianity," writes:

> It is when I turn to Christ, when I give myself up to His Personality, that I first begin to have a real personality of my own. At the beginning I said there were Personalities in God. I will go further now. There are no real personalities anywhere else. Until you have given yourself to Him you will not have a real self... You must throw it away 'blindly' so to speak. Christ will indeed give you a real personality

. . . The very first step is to try to forger about the self altogether. Your real, new self (which is Christ's and also yours, and yours just because it is His) . . . . It will come when you are looking for Him. Give up yourself, and you will find your real self. Lose your life and you will save it. Submit to death, death of your ambitions and favourite wishes every day and death of your whole body in the end: submit with every fibre of your being, and you will find eternal life. Keep back nothing. Nothing that you have not given away will be really yours. Nothing in you that has not died will ever be raised from the dead. Look for yourself, and you will find in that long run only hatred, loneliness, despair, rage, ruin, and decay. But look for Christ and you will find Him, and with Him everything else thrown in.[13]

He is our everything and all things needed we can find at His table of salvation. This is what Francis Thompson sought for and finally found in his great work, "The Hound Of Heaven." An excerpted portion follows:

THE HOUND OF HEAVEN

I fled Him, down the nights and down the days;
I fled Him, down the arches of the years;
I fled Him, down the labyrinthine ways
Of my own mind; and in the midst of tears
I hid from Him, and under running laughter.

Up visited homes, I sped;

---

[13] Clives Staples Lewis, Mere Christianity, (C.S. Lewis Pte. Ltd. Copyright 1980.) pp. 226-227.

And shot precipitated,
Adown Titanic glooms of chasmed fears,
From those strong Feet that followed, followed after.

But with unhurrying chase,
And unperturbed pace,
Deliberate speed, majestic instancy,
They beat – and a Voice beat,
More instant than the Feet:
"All things betray thee, who betrayest Me."

Now of that long pursuit
Comes on at hand the bruit;
That Voice is round me like a bursting sea:
"And is thy earth so marred,
Shattered in shard on shard?
Lo, all things fly thee, for thou fliest Me!

Strange, piteous, futile thing!
Wherefore should any set thee love apart?
Seeing none but I makes much of naught" (He said),
"And human love needs human meriting:
How hast thou merited –
Of all Man's clotted clay, the dingiest clot?
Alack! Thou knewest not
How little worthy of any love thou art!
Whom wilt thou find to love ignoble thee,
Save Me, save only Me?

All which I took from thee, I did but take,
Not for thy harms,
But just that thou might'st seek it in my arms
All which thy child's mistake
Fancies as lost, I have stored for thee at home:

Rise, clasp My hand, and come!"
Halts by me that footfall.
Is my gloom after all,
Shade of His hand, outstretched caressingly?
"Ah, fondest, blindest, weakest,
I am He who thou seekest!
Thou dravest Love from thee, who dravest Me.[14]

-Francis Thompson

---

[14] An excerpt from Francis Thompson's, the Hound of Heaven (New York: McCracken Press, 1993)

SANCTIFICATION[15]

I would like to view this act of grace which we call sanctification from a cyclical view point. There has been much written of this act from differing and varied positions. I believe that we should view sanctification as one of the many acts we receive once we become a believer. The Apostle Paul writes his God inspired defense of our position in grace in his letter to the Galatians 6:14:

> **But God forbid that I should boast except in the cross of our Lord Jesus Christ, by whom the world has been crucified to me, and I to the world.**

The finished work of the cross is and must be the centerpiece of all interpretation of the divine. The finished work of the cross must have preeminence in our understanding and learning. It must be placed first in our accomplishment and desire. Paul uses the optative, *genoito* from the Greek, *ginomai* and with the negative, *me* means 'no indeed!' which we translate 'God forbid' making that statement a wish or a desire. It becomes almost a prayer that he may never glory in anything save the cross. I think this is significant. We must place our Lord and what He did on the cross and His resurrection above all.

In our salvation experience, we become as a large tree. We grow from the roots upward into a mighty creation of the Lord affixed with the many acts, gifts and fruits growing from our trunk of salvation.

---

[15] This chapter, "Sanctification," was originally titled, "The Cycle of Sanctification," and was originally published in my earlier work, "Concerning the Christ." Published by FWB Publishing. c. 2011

Our roots that anchor us into the ground are twofold. Our first root is Scripture. The word of God. The communication from God the Son. The second root is the Holy Spirit, God the Spirit. These two divine roots anchor our trunk of salvation and will keep us in the ground no matter the sway of dissenting and differing opinions that may cross our paths.

From our trunk of salvation our limbs will grow. These limbs are the acts of the Holy Spirit. Sanctification is one such limb. Sanctification is the process of the Holy Spirit changing the believer more and more into the image of the Lord, God the Son. In this process, we are set apart and aside for God's will and worship and service. We must grab hold of this act and allow its power to transform the believer. We must transform our form to conform to His form to paraphrase Romans 12. In Colossians 2:4-10 we read:

Now this I say lest anyone should deceive you with persuasive words. For though I am absent in the flesh, yet I am with you in spirit, rejoicing   to see your good order and the steadfastness of your faith in Christ. As you therefore have received Christ Jesus the Lord, so walk in Him, rooted and built up in Him and established in   the faith, as you have been taught abounding in it with thanksgiving. Beware lest anyone cheat you through philosophy and empty deceit, according to the tradition of men, according to   the basic principles of the world, and not according to Christ. For in Him, dwells all the fullness of the Godhead bodily; and you are complete in Him, who is the head of all principality and power.

We are able to begin to explain our cycle of sanctification. In Christ, we discover that we obtain our *Position* in sanctification. A position is defined as our situation or condition with relation to a circumstance. A position is a status or standing. A position is the location or place of a person at a given moment. When a person is converted to the Lord and is a believer, he is sanctified. We are situated in sanctification due to our circumstance of salvation. We have a status or standing in Christ not due us, but due to Him. We are complete in Him. A person might offer and say that Scripture implies we are to do something in this act of grace which we have termed sanctification and I agree. This doing is part and participatory of this cycle and will be addressed in this chapter. But for now at the beginning of this short and non-exhaustive explanation, we believers EXIST in sanctification because of the Lord and His grace and are complete in the fruition of what He did at Calvary and His resurrection.

The Apostle Paul writes in his introduction of 1 Corinthians 1:2:

> **To the church of God which is at Corinth, to those who are sanctified in Christ Jesus, called   to   be saints, with all who in every place call on the name of Jesus Christ our Lord, both theirs and ours. . .**

Jude in his very Jewish Christian letter in verse 1 writes:

> **To those who are called, sanctified by God the Father, and preserved in Jesus Christ. . .**

A third example of this existence and position is given in Hebrews 2:10-11:

For it was fitting for Him, for whom are all things and by whom are all things, in bringing many sons to glory, to make the captain of their salvation perfect through sufferings. For both He who sanctifies and those who are being sanctified are all of one, for which reason He is not ashamed to call them brethren. . .

Because of our position in Christ the Lord Jesus, we have an active and subjective sanctification. We live and reside and stand in a sanctified state via salvation. We are the subject of an act of grace we call sanctification by our position as a believer. Under the great covering umbrella of grace, we receive this position. We, as believers, heirs and joint heirs with the Lord can claim that we in an active sense, a nounal sense, a concrete existing sense, in a subjective sense are not what we were, but are now living in a state of sanctification. We are being set apart for worship and service to and for God. We have become as Paul has written in 2 Corinthians 5:17, a new creation. We are existential in our position with Christ as sanctified. The first stop on our cycle of sanctification is *Positional Sanctification.*

The second point on this cycle is *Pragmatic Sanctification.* Sanctification as an act of grace from our Lord is very pragmatic and practical. Webster defines Philosophical Pragmaticism as the philosophical system stressing practical consequences as constituting the essential criterion in determining truth or value. I wish to apply this definition to our topic. To live and exist in sanctification must demonstrate an altering change within the believer. While sanctification is existential, it is also experiential. We EXPERIENCE this process of making us more and more like Him and less and less like ourselves. He, the Lord is our imitation, our pattern. In 1 Corinthians 11:1 we read:

. . . imitate me as I imitate the Lord . . .

Paul writes further in Ephesians 5:1:

Therefore be imitators of God as dear children.

Once saved the believer is posited in sanctification, but also is living in sanctification by both his action and state of being. This pragmatic is verbal as it concerns the language of becoming more and more like the Lord. This language of sanctification makes our understanding of our existence and further experience as Christians more real and posits us into the truth which is found in totality in the work of the Lord Jesus Christ for He is truth.

In our Positional Sanctification, we are sanctified by the Lord. In our Pragmatic Sanctification we grow more sanctified and experience it. This is not a contradiction. It is demonstrative of the process of growing in the Lord and becoming a mature Christian. We not only are *because of Him*. We are now experiencing the gift of being *in Him*.

The Apostle Paul talks of this pragmatism in Romans 6:19 and 22:

. . . For just as you presented your members as slaves of uncleanness, and of lawlessness leading to more lawlessness, so now present your members as slaves of righteousness for holiness.

But now having been set free from sin, and having becomes slaves of God, you have your fruit to holiness, and the end, everlasting life.

The truth of the matter is that during our Christian walk we are not our own. We are not the determiner of our position or pragmatic in our walk of life. As a Christian we are slaves to God in holiness and are sanctified or set apart for the worship of Him. He is the determiner of our path. I fear that modern Christianity has ignored and forgotten this truth demonstrated by the axiom, 'God is because He is and we are because He is.' We are His slaves. Before conversion and the coming to faith, we were slaves to sin and apart and away from God. As Christian we are subjects to the King and He is our master. As slaves we are to do our master's bidding. We must put off the old man and put on the new man. The Lord makes provision for us in this matter by first giving us our sanctification and then instituting the process for us to become more and more sanctified. As we have stated previously, for us to be more and more like Him.

The cycle of sanctification continues to revolve for it is truly a revolution. It is the process of altering us into becoming who He would have us. Our Positional Sanctification and our Pragmatic Sanctification in turn leads us to our *Progressive Sanctification*. The Greek word, *hagiasmos* which we translate sanctification bespeaks and implies a process, a progression or growth toward a holy or consecrated state in our worship of and for the Lord. We, in our action and state of being affix and attest sanctification in our walk and life. This occurrence layers an attributive modification to the believer. The person as he once was is exposed in his deficiency. This EXPOSITION of the person must modify him to become more like the Lord. An exposition through Christ. An exposing of the believer through Christ. Our sanctification is not only *because of Him* and *in Him*, but is *through Him*. An exposition is the uncovering, the baring, the exhibition, the making known and the revelation of something or somebody. Exposition also means to subject something or somebody to an influence or action. As believers we can never be the same as we once were after we are altered by the sanctifying power of the Lord.

In 1 Peter 2:9-10 we read:

But you are chosen generation, a royal priesthood, a holy nation, His own special people, that you may proclaim the praises of Him who called you out of darkness into His marvelous light; who once were not a people   but are now the people of God, who had not obtained mercy but now have obtained mercy.

We are chosen being set apart. We are a royal priesthood being set apart. We are a holy nation being set apart. We are His own special people being set apart. We proclaim His praises being set apart. We are called being set apart. We are the people of God being set apart. We have obtained mercy being set apart. The attributes of the Christian include a sanctified existence, experience and exposition of a once sinful man and now a believer of the Lord. The Apostle Paul writes in 1 Thessalonians 4:7-8:

For God did not call us to uncleanness, but in holiness. Therefore he who rejects this does not reject man, but God, who has also given us His Holy Spirit.

The Greek word for holiness, *hagios* is the same root word for sanctification, *hagiasmos*. If we are posited in sanctity and holiness and our pragmatic is sanctity and holiness then our progression must also be sanctity and holiness. We are to be holy as He is holy. We must be clean in our imitation of Him. This is one of the primary tasks of God the Spirit. He is to present the believers as a chaste bride to the Groom, the Lord Jesus Christ. Our chastity is arrived and progresses in the Lord through God the Spirit.

I offer this crude analogy to clarify my point. If a person becomes a fisherman, he must first decide to become a fisherman. He calls himself a fisherman. He then starts to act as a fisherman. He puts on the attributes and characteristics and mannerisms of a fisherman. He begins to walk and talk as a fisherman. The traits acquired might not have been part of his former behavior. His demeanor becomes altered. To become a complete fisherman, he had to go through a life changing and spirit changing and soul changing experience. He had to start acting as a fisherman acts. His state of being was that of a fisherman. He was altered and more and more he walked, talked, behaved and concerned himself as a fisherman. This is not only intellectual, but also in his heart and soul. Slowly and methodically and eventually he inevitably becomes more the fisherman and less the non-fisherman. This is the universal method present is any situation of growth within a human person. It is also present in our becoming more like the Lord in our imitation of Him and being set apart for worship of a holy God.

Progressive Sanctification is the activity within the cycle of sanctification that modifies and alters the believer from what he was into what the Lord would have us be. Pardon my rehearsals and repetitions. I do not think that one can repeat certain matters enough. Repetition is a key foundation in our learning process. Perhaps a new thing at first is alien to our ears, but we can soon understand it by going over and rereading the material concerning the issue at hand.

If our position in sanctification is an active subject of language within the cycle and our pragmatic sanctification is verbal in that we grow and live in a state of being called sanctification then our progressive sanctification is adjectival. It is the modification of our walk with the Lord. We are altered into His image. We grow. We mature.

A fourth point found on this cycle that we enjoy in grace is our *Phenomenal Sanctification*. A phenomenon is a fact, an occurrence or circumstance observed. It is something remarkable or extraordinary. In the cycle of sanctification, it is the making holy by an external force. It this case, that force is the Lord. It is an EVENT in our Christian walk that is done by God. It is a happening.

We have seen the working of the Holy Spirit, God the Spirit in our lives; in the subjective, our existence and position and the verbal, our experience and pragmatic and the adjectival, our exposition and progression and we also see the working of the objective, our event and phenomenon in the Lord. This event occurs *by Him*. The Apostle Paul in 2 Thessalonians 2:13-15 writes:

But we are bound to give thanks to God always for you, brethren beloved by the Lord, because God from the beginning chose you for salvation through sanctification by the Spirit and belief in the truth, to which He called you by our gospel, for the obtaining of the glory of our Lord Jesus Christ. Therefore, brethren, stand fast and hold the traditions which you were taught, whether by word or our epistle.

Sanctification is an act of grace that the Lord does for and to us. Sanctification is always part and participatory of our imitation of the Lord. This act of grace is divine in its origin. This act is the method of making us holy as He is holy. To reach for the divine and abandon the mortal, we require and need the work of the divine to pattern ourselves like He is. With all the descriptions we have utilized to attempt to demonstrate sanctification, we must add the words objective and passive.

This act is not only subjective, verbal and adjectival, but also objective. This act is done to us by the divine.

This act is not only active as in Positional Sanctification, but also passive in Phenomenal Sanctification. We are passive as it is the work of the Holy Spirit when we become believers in His truth, the gospel (re. 1 Corinthians 15:1-4). When we became saved, the purpose of this act is our glorification of the Lord.

We see the interaction of the entire cycle of sanctification by these three verses. Sanctification is not a static point, but a revolution, a cycle of interaction of the subject and the verbal and the modifying adjectival and the objective. This act further demonstrates that we are both active and passive in its working.

This cycle of language displays the framing of the reality in that it is achieved because of the Lord, in the Lord, through the Lord and by the Lord. He is our truth and we grow more like His truth and become more like His truth and He covers us in and with His truth. Sanctification is not a onetime event, but a continuing imitation of the Lord in our existence and experience and exposition and in the eventful will of the Lord. Paul continues to write of this phenomenon in Romans 15:14-17:

> **Now I myself am confident concerning you, my brethren, that you also are full of goodness, filled with all knowledge, able also to admonish one another. Nevertheless, brethren, I have written more boldly to you on some points, as reminding you, because of the grace given to me by God, that I might be a minister of Jesus Christ to the Gentiles, ministering the gospel of God that the offering of the Gentiles might be acceptable, sanctified by the Holy Spirit. Therefore I have reason to glory in Christ Jesus in the things which pertain to God.**

Phenomenal Sanctification is the descriptive of what the Holy Spirit, the Lord and the God the Father do to the believer. We are the object of this act. We are the passive of this act being accomplished within us. God does the work in this event to make us acceptable to Him.

In conclusion of this short overview of the complex work of sanctification in a believer's life, let me restate that sanctification is a cycle, a revolution. It must not be observed lineally which might give rise to the opportunity for spiritual myopia, spiritual nearsightedness. The nearsightedness of seeing only one static point present on the entire cycle and drawing a conclusion from this stasis and not seeing the entire cycle.

This cycle of sanctification is interactive. The cycle grows and matures and revolves and continues during the Christian walk. We find Scripture displaying and depicting the interaction between our position and pragmatic: Acts 20:32, 26:18, 1 Corinthians 6:11, Hebrews 10:14 and Ephesians 5:26. We see the evolvement of sanctification between the pragmatic and the progressive: Hebrews 12:14, 1 Peter 1:2 and 3:15, 1 Thessalonians 4:3-4 and John 17:17 and 19. Between the progressive and the phenomenal: Hebrews 9:11-15 and 13:12. Lastly, between the phenomenal and the positional: 1 Corinthians 1:30, 1 Thessalonians 5:23 and Hebrews 10:10.

Sanctification, the process of becoming holy, of becoming more and more like the Lord. Necessary, of course. Given, thankfully. Applied, mercifully. Graciously, the act of the Lord upon His believers. Sanctification is the hallmark of the Christian. It is a cycle of maturing in the Lord. In this act of sanctification, I cannot help but be reminded of that poem by St. Patrick, "The Breastplate." This poem symbolizes our walk and work in and due the Lord and is offered in excerpt:

THE BREASTPLATE

Christ shield me today
Against poison,
Against burning,
Against drowning,
Against wounding,
So that there may come to me abundance of reward,
Christ with me,
Christ before me,
Christ behind me,
Christ in me,
Christ beneath me,
Christ above me,
Christ on my right,
Christ on my left,
Christ when I lie down,
Christ when I sit down
Christ when I arise,
Christ in quiet,
Christ in danger,
Christ in the heart of every man, who thinks of me,
Christ in the mouth of everyone who speaks of me,
Christ in every eye that sees me,
Christ in every ear that hears me,
-St. Patrick

The Lord Jesus Christ is our sanctification. The Holy Spirit orchestrates and accomplishes our sanctification. The glorification of God the Father in making chaste and acceptable a bride for the Groom, God the Son via the act of God the Spirit is the purpose of sanctification. Oh my what a God we serve.

SEVEN STANZAS AT EASTER

Make no mistake: if He rose at all
it was as His body.
if the cells' dissolution did not reverse,
the molecules reknit, the amino acids rekindle,
the Church will fall.
It was not as the flowers,
each soft Spring recurrent;
If was not as His Spirit
in the mouths and fuddled eyes of the eleven apostles;
it was as His flesh: ours.
The same hinged thumbs and toes,
the same valved heart
that-pierced-died, withered, paused,
and then regathered out of enduring Might
new strength to enclose.
Let us not mock God with metaphor,
analogy, sidestepping, transcendence;
making of the event a parable,
a sign painted in the faded credulity of earlier ages:
let us walk through the door.
The stone is rolled back, not papier-mâché,
not stone in a story,
but the vast rock of materiality
that in the slow grinding of time will eclipse for each of us
the wide light of day.
And if we will have an angel at the tomb,
make it a real angel,
weighty with Max Planck's quanta, vivid with hair,
opaque in the dawn light,
robed in real linen spun on a definite loom.

Let us not seek to make it less monstrous,
for our own convenience, our own sense of beauty,
lest, awakened in one unthinkable hour,
we are embarrassed by the miracle,
and crushed by remonstrance.[16]

-John Updike

---

[16] John Updike, Telephone Poles and Other Poems, c. 1961 by John Updike, Reprinted by Dr. John W. Montgomery, *"The Suicide of Christian Theology"* (Newburgh, IN: Trinity Press, 1970) pp.40-41

FAITH[17]

CREDE UT INTELLIGAS –Anselm

'Believe that you may know'

INTELLIGE UT CREDAS –Abelard

'Know that you may believe'

What is faith? To many in our world, this is the proverbial million dollar question. Faith is defined as: having confidence or trust in a person or thing, belief in God, a system of religious belief, loyalty or fidelity. In the Greek language, the word we translate as faith is *pistis* and the word for belief is a verbal form of that same word, *pisteuo.* Epistemology is the academic study of truth and knowledge. To me faith, belief and truth are akin to each other and interchangeable in the theological sense. Both Saints Anselm and Abelard have, in a lineal fashion captured to a certain degree what faith, belief and truth and knowledge are. St. Anselm held you must start your journey with belief. God is and therefore you may know. Saint Abelard held that you must start your journey with the knowledge of the existence of God and then you may believe. Both held that there is both knowledge and belief, but they maintained opposite starting points. Faith is a cycle and thus must be defined as a cycle.

---

[17] This chapter, "Faith," was originally titled, "The Cycle of Faith," and was originally published in my earlier work, "Concerning the Christ. Published by FWB Publishing. c. 2011.

Cyclically, faith is more than the belief of the knowledge of God or the knowledge of one's belief in God. Faith, what a person holds to be true is more, in the ultimate eternal sense than the assent of the intellect to revealed truth. It is the practical submission of the entire man to the guidance and control of truth. Our faith must find its truth in our submission to God.

In this age of grace, it is our believing in the truth of the finished work of the cross; the death, burial and resurrection of the Lord Jesus Christ.

Our faith, our saving faith, is more than simple believeism. Many stand or kneel and cry that they believe, but do they believe in the finished work of the cross. Many believe in this or that. Many believe and hold to be true a particular denomination or rite or gift. They hold that they are saved by these things. In the Jewish Christian epistle written by the Apostle James, the Lord's half-brother chapter 2:19 we read that even the demons believe and tremble. We must submit in order to be believers and are saved when we trust and believe and know the truth of the finished work of God the Son, Jesus Christ.

Faith, in its totality of definition, speaks of and describes our interaction with whomever or whatever a person believes in. Who or what they believe to be true. That faith will define a person. That faith becomes an explanation of truth by which a person will cling to and therefore order his or her life. That faith will reflect how a person understands his or her universe. Faith is the word that we as English speakers have garnered to communicate the concept of what is real to a person.

Faith is more than an acknowledgement of an existential or experiential moment or notion in a person's life. In the Christian sense, faith is the cycle of the EXISTENTIAL, EXPERIENTIAL, EXPOSITIONAL and the EVENTFUL with the Lord. In this cycle of faith, the Lord becomes our reality and foundation. In the Christian experience, our faith and what we hold to be true is the God of Scripture which has been spoken by God the Son and inspired by God the Spirit. We exist in this truth that the Lord has given to us by His grace. We have faith in His finished work of the cross and during this time of the age of grace we know the truth that He died for our sins, He was buried in holiness and He rose the third day as the First fruits of the resurrection. Beginning here, we exist by faith and we now can experience our faith and grow and mature in our Lord. Our faith, our knowledge that He is true will grow and we will become more faithful. This exposing of our lack of faith will cause us to be more faithful in our imitation of the Lord. As we grow more faithful, the Lord will make us experience faith by events in our life which will allow us to have a richer and deeper faith. This is the same cycle as written above in the Cycle of Sanctification, but is utilized concerning the concept of the Cycle of Faith.

THE PROCESS OF THE CYCLE

In our existing in faith, we are the subject of faith. It is what a person believes to be true. It is what a person knows to be true. In the Christian sense, a person must believe, trust and know that He is the Lord and what He did on Calvary, Romans 10:9-13. This is the beginning of all truth, of all saving truth. This faith is the subjective active nounal position of our cycle. It is tangible in the salvation experience. This is an arbitrary choice. What do you believe to true?

All cycles are interactive as a sphere where one point touches another and makes the whole of the sphere complete. This is true within the Cycle of Faith.

Therefore the subjective active position of our existence is then verbally experienced in a pragmatic way. We grow in our faith.

Adjectivally, our faith, by our growth, exposes the believer and his or her lack of faith into a more progressive faith.

Through the work of the Holy Spirit, we undergo events in our life in an objective passive phenomenal eventful manner.

The Greek word *pistis* is the word found within the New Testament we English speakers translate by the word faith as mentioned previously. Faith is defined as to have allegiance and belief and trust in God. In the Pauline influenced letter, Hebrews 11:1-2 the writer writes:

> **Now faith is the substance of things hoped for, the evidence of things not seen. For by it the elders obtained a good testimony**.

The word 'substance' in the Greek language is the word, *hupostasis*. One definition of this word is substance, but another can be 'foundation'. What a wonderful rendering of a powerful word. Faith is our foundation. Like a house, faith is what we build and experience our belief upon. The Greek literally suggests that faith is the means by which we can stand. Another definition for this word is 'reality'. By faith or what we would hold to be true, we frame the reality of our world view. It is the evidence and proof of those things we have not seen. One adage for faith is the seeing the end of road before one has begun the journey. Faith takes on the definition of knowledge and trust in a truth outside of oneself.   Within the traditional orthodox Christian context, God must be the object of our faith. He is the truth outside of our self in whom we hold and known as true. In Him we rest and by no other person or ism or schism. Only in and through Him. The writer of Hebrews continues in chapter 11:6:

> **But without faith it is impossible to please Him, for he who comes to God must believe that He is, and that He is a rewarder of those who diligently seek Him.**

Once a person has come to the table of salvation, faith becomes an attribute of the person who would call upon the Lord. In 2 Timothy 2:22, we read:

> **Flee   also   youthful   lusts;   but   pursue righteousness, faith, love, peace with those who call on the Lord out of a pure heart.**

At salvation we have faith, but faith in turn leads to more faith. We become more rock sure of our truth in the finished work of the cross as we grow in the Lord. Paul continues in chapter 4:7 that our faith is tangible and can be kept:

> **I have fought the good fight, I have finished the race, I have kept the faith**.

Our faith must be as real and viable as a fight or a race. Faith as a noun must be as tangible as a person, place or thing.

In its verbal form, faith is translated belief, *pisteuo*. To believe means: to be persuaded of a thing, to give credit to, to have confidence in, to trust. As we have mentioned earlier in this work, a verb is an action or a state of mine or being. In the construction of reality, what we have been subject to is what we do or what we reside within by our existence and through our experience. Faith in action is belief. Faith once achieved is our state of being. The Apostle Paul wrote to Timothy that, "I have kept the faith." Can we not also translate this passage, "I have kept the pledge," or "I have trusted in the truth of God?"

Faith rendered in its adjectival form is faithful. The Greek language has a form for this adjective. It is the word, *pistos*. It is defined as to be trustworthy, faithful to a promise. In further translating of 2 Timothy 4:7, we can translate Paul to read, "I have been faithful to the promise."

The obvious question that now arises is what or who is the promise. In the Christian context, the promise is and can only be the Lord Jesus Christ and His gospel, His message. He becomes our reality. He becomes our foundation. He becomes the One we build our house of truth upon in order for us to live in His presence. He is to whom we make our pledge. He is to whom we trust as our truth. His gospel; wherein we live with Him in His death upon a cross where He became sin for us, His burial where we are buried with Him in the ground in holiness and His resurrection where we arise with Him from the tomb in new life with the power of God unto salvation. This is our vicarious, substitutionary atonement.

We are not only the subject of faith, though we are. We not experience belief, though we do. We do not only become more faithful in our progression, though we must. Faith is also what God gives to us as a believer in Him. There is a voice of language in Greek called the passive voice. We can write and say in the active, "I like dogs." In the passive voice, we can say, "I am liked by dogs." In the second example, the subject is being liked by the dogs. The subject has become the object of the action of the verb and the object is the one doing the action in the oblique prepositional phrase. I offer this crude example of the passive voice to illustrate that we can be the object of something outside of ourselves. A form of the word 'faith' in the Greek language is found in this type of construction. In the New Testament, the verb *pistoo* is only found in the passive voice. It linguistically morphs when in the passive voice from *pistoo* and becomes *epistothen*.

In the English language it means, to be assured or to be made faithful. God not only posits us with faith in our existence. God not only allows us to be pragmatic and experience faith as belief as we grow. God not only allows us to progress and expose our deficiencies in order that we may become more faithful, but God gives us the phenomenon or event from Him thus making us to be faithful. We see this complete cycle in Paul's writing 2 Timothy 3:14-15:

> **But you must continue in the things which you have learned and been assured of, knowing from whom you have learned them, and that from childhood you have known the Holy Scriptures, which are able to make you wise for salvation through faith which is in Christ Jesus.**

In continuing our cyclical model we have utilized throughout this book, we have faith, belief, faithful and to be made faithful. In the Greek language, we have *pistis*, *pisteuo*, *pistos* and *epistothen*. We can see our existence, experience, exposition and event of faith. We can see our position, our pragmatic, our progression and our phenomenon of faith. We can see the process; the cycle of maturation we call faith. I understand that the tenor, the tone of the cited Scripture concerns itself with the importance of Scripture, but we still can see the cycle given to Timothy from Paul via the Holy Spirit. Timothy, a man of and with faith. Paul writes:

You must continue in the things: The Greek word *mene* meaning to remain or abide

To have belief and reside in faith. To believe.

You have learned: The Greek *emathes* from the word *manthano* meaning to learn

To have belief. To believe.

And you have been assured of: This is the passive voice of pistoo, *epistothes* and in this construction means that Timothy is being assured of something by someone or something outside of himself.

To be made faithful.

Knowing of whom: This is the participle form of *oida*, *eidos* meaning to know.

To have belief.

You have learned them: Again the word, *emathes*, to learn.

To believe. To have belief. To be faithful.

You have known the Holy Scriptures: The Greek word *oidas*, to know.

To have faith.

Which are able: The Greek word *dunamena*, meaning to be able.

To have faith.

To make you wise: The infinitive, *sophisais*, meaning to be wise.

To be made faithful.

Unto salvation: The preposition *eis*, meaning unto or into.

To have faith.

Through faith: The preposition *dia*, meaning through or by means of.

To believe. To be faithful. To be made faithful

Which is in Christ Jesus: The foundation of Timothy's faith, belief, faithfulness and the giver of faith.

The apostle Paul continues concerning this process of faith later in chapter 2:16-17:

> **All Scripture is given by inspiration of God, and is profitable for doctrine, for reproof, for correction, for instruction in righteousness, that the man of God may be complete, thoroughly equipped for every good work.**

In verse 16, we read this cycle of faith is the method through the Word, the Scripture of God that leads the believer into verse 17. In verse 17, after the cycle of faith has revolved, the believer is complete and ready for the work of God. Complete not in the sense of being finished for all cycles of grace are a revolution including this cycle of grace, faith. Faith continues on, always cyclical and depicting the further maturation of the believer. He will become useful and then more useful being rigged with what is necessary for the task at hand. He will be and will become more Christ like. A. W. Tozer writes:

> Jesus Christ is enough for all our needs. He is our great High Priest and intercessor in heaven. He is the worthy Lamb of God. By His blood He has consecrated forever the way into God's presence. He is our man in glory. Let us thankfully hide in Him and be safe.

We have faith in God as Christians. We reside and abide in our belief in God and the finished work of the Lord; His death, burial and resurrection. We grow and become more faithful in our belief we trust in. God, graciously, appropriates to us more faith in the truth that He is. This cycle of grace of faith allows to us the reality of a sovereign, holy, immutable, loving and infinite God to strengthen and equip and reconcile a fallen mankind back to Himself. God becomes our reality and foundation upon whom we as believers can safely rest.

A SUFFICIENT GRACE

I THEN SHALL LIVE
Lyrics by Gloria Gaither and music by Jean Sibelius[18]

I THEN SHALL LIVE AS ONE WHO'S BEEN FORGIVEN;
I'LL WALK WITH JOY TO KNOW MY DEBTS ARE PAID.
I KNOW MY NAME IS CLEAR BEFORE MY FATHER;
I AM HIS CHILD, AND I AM NOT AFRAID.
SO GREATLY PARDONED, I'LL FORGIVE MY BROTHER.
THE LAW OF LOVE I GLADLY WILL OBEY.

I THEN SHALL LIVE AS ONE WHO'S LEARNED COMPASSION;
I'VE BEEN SO LOVED THAT I'LL RISK LOVING TOO.
I KNOW HOW FEAR BUILDS WALLS INSTEAD OF BRIDGES;
I'LL DARE TO SEE ANOTHER'S POINT OF VIEW.
AND WHEN RELATIONSHIP DEMANDS COMMITMENT,
THEN I'LL BE THERE TO CARE AND FOLLOW THROUGH.

YOUR KINGDOM COME AROUND AND THROUGH AND IN
ME;
YOUR POWER AND GLORY LET THEM SHINE THROUGH ME;
YOUR HALLOWED NAME, O MAY I BEAR WITH HONOR.
AND MAY YOUR LIVING KINGDOM COME IN ME.
THE BREAD OF LIFE, O MAY I SHARE WITH HONOR,
AND MAY YOU FEED A HUNGRY WORLD THROUGH ME.

AMEN. AMEN. AMEN.

---

[18] "I Then Shall Live," lyrics by Gloria Gaither. Music by Jean Sibelius. Words c. Warner/Chappell Music, Inc. Universal Music Publishing Group.

I CAN ONLY IMAGINE
by Bart Mallard[19]

I CAN ONLY IMAGINE WHAT IT WILL BE LIKE
WHEN I WALK BY YOUR SIDE
I CAN ONLY IMAGINE WHAT MY EYES WILL SEE
WHEN YOUR FACE IS BEFORE ME
I CAN ONLY IMAGINE

SURROUNDED BY YOUR GLORY, WHAT WILL MY HEART
FEEL
WILL I DANCE FOR YOU JESUS OR IN AWE OF YOU BE STILL
WILL I STAND IN YOUR PRESENCE OR TO MY KNEES WILL I
FALL
WILL I SING HALLELUJAH, WILL I BE ABLE TO SPEAK AT ALL
I CAN ONLY IMAGINE, I CAN ONLY IMAGE

I CAN ONLY IMAGINE WHEN THAT DAY COMES
AND I FIND MYSELF STANDING IN THE SON
I CAN ONLY IMAGINE WHEN ALL I WILL DO
IS FOREVER, FOREVER WORSHIP YOU
I CAN ONLY IMAGINE

I CAN ONLY IMAGINE, I CAN ONLY IMAGE

I CAN ONLY IMAGINE WHEN ALL I WILL DO
IS FOREVER, FOREVER WORSHIP YOU

---

[19] "I Can Only Imagine," by Bart Mallard. Simpleville Music (ASCAP), c. 2001, 2002.

As I begin this essay I am overwhelmed by internal thoughts of both folly and arrogance. Who am I to even consider voicing an opinion on this topic when so many great leaders of the church and scholars of the precious word of the Lord have broached this subject for over two millennia? Augustine of Hippo, Boethius, John Calvin, Jacob Arminius, and many others during their mortality have dipped their toes into the icy water of thought and then dived into the deep water head first into controversy and thought. Deep and perilous water with vicious and dangerous cresting waves of theology and philosophy wait concerning a topic guaranteed to present the seeker to the criticism and scorn of others entrenched within a particular point of view of doctrine. Those two affirming and also alienating words of Predestination and Free-will which cause an argument between so many Christians. A seemingly either/or situation by so many over so many years of argument and division. I believe that in reality and totality the seeming division is a both/and situation and will be discussed later in this essay. I am only a novice and just a lay person when compared to the giants who have preceded me. I start this work and dip my toe into the current and prepare to plunge into the depths.

The fear of the Lord is the instruction of wisdom, and before honor is humility.[20]

I am the true vine, and My Father is the vinedresser. Every branch in Me that does not bear fruit He takes away: and every branch that bears fruit He prunes, that it may bear more fruit. You

---

[20] Proverbs 15:33, The New King James Version (NKJV).

are already clean because of the word which I have spoken to you. Abide in Me, and I in you. As the branch cannot bear fruit of itself, unless it abides in the vine, neither can you, unless you abide in Me. I am the vine, you are the branches. He who abides in Me, and I in him, bears much fruit; for without Me you can do nothing.[21]

The primary method by which I will present my argument is one of an accumulative nature. I will, like the proverbial wall painter apply with varied and multiple strokes upon our wall of understanding. In the course of time, perhaps I can reach a conclusion concerning this far-reaching and wide-scoped disagreement of varying points of view within and without the Christian community. In the end, I wish to have painted my wall of discourse completely and smoothly with a logic and completeness of thought. I ask before-hand the reader's patience and forbearance if I may come across disjointed or a hodge-podge for a time. My goal is that by the end of this work, we, the reader and the author may achieve common ground concerning the debate between Predestination and Free-will.

THE REST OF THE STORY

During much of the second half of the twentieth century there was a radio commentator who had a great following in the United States of America. His name was Paul Harvey.[22] Mr. Harvey would broadcast several times a

---

[21] The Gospel of John 15:1-5
[22] Mr. Paul Harvey, radio personality and commentator. B. 1918. D. 2009

day and on one on-going series, he had segments which would begin with a teaser. He then would come to the climax of the story and Mr. Harvey would give the climax and state, "And now you know the rest of the story." His broadcasts were always pithy and illuminating.

The topic of this lay discussion is the topic and the controversy concerning the theological points of view of Predestination/Eternal Security and Free-Will/Backsliding. It is, in a Christian context the argument between a doctrinal position labelled Calvinism from John Calvin and an opposing position called Arminianism from Jacob Arminius. Much of the Protestant world have opinions and doctrines concerning this topic. Some advocate the one and eviscerate the other. Millions of Christian believers have entrenched and staunch views. To these believers it is an either/or proposition. The theme and direction of this work will be a both/and approach. I do not believe or understand this argument must be one way or the other. I hold that in actuality it is both. I maintain a Capatabilistic approach concerning this matter in discussion.

If I have not alienated you with my previous statement and you have not thrown my work into a circular file, I will continue on for a bit.

A GENERAL PARADIGM

I believe all of the Lord's believers hold to be true that He has all creation under His control. He has a plan. It is His plan and responds to His command as do we all. From before time and worlds and universes, He has always been

God. He, by definition must and will always transcend the limitations we have as mortals. Created beings breathing His air and living under His all-knowing providence and sovereignty might place on our experiences an attempt to understand and control our situation. None the less we must always take the proverbial deep breath and recognize we demonstrate little in the presence of a holy and omnipotent God. The most hyper-Calvinist and the most ardent Arminian must bow to the mediating fact that He is God and we are not. May I add thankfully we are not God?

The first section of our paradigm which I offer is that He has a plan. He has always had a plan. His plan is indeed predestined by the Triune God in His determinate counsel of His council before anything or anyone.[23] Those who reside in their frame of reference on the Arminian side may shirk away from that word, Predestination, but that word only means: that which was fated before. The Triune God would never be nor could ever be taken by surprise. He knew how this plan was to unfold before the first matter of the universe was spoken into existence. From the outset of this work, let me state that I will use terms that certain groups have taken and used for a narrow and myopic position. Predestination is just one of the terms in which I wish to use in their original definition.

The Apostle Paul writes under the inspiration of the Holy Spirit of a portion of God's plan in his first letter to the Corinthian Church:

---

[23] The Acts of the Apostles 2:23

> **But now Christ is risen from the dead, and has become the Firstfruits of those who have fallen asleep. For since by man came death, by Man also came the resurrection of the dead. For as in Adam all die, even so in Christ all shall be made alive. But each one in his own order: Christ the Firstfruits, afterward those who are Christ's at His coming. Then comes the end, when He delivers the kingdom to God the Father, when He puts an end to all rule and all authority and power. For He must reign till He has put all enemies under His feet. The last enemy that will be destroyed is death. "For He has put all things under His feet."[24] But when He says "all things are put under Him," it is evident that He who put all things under Him is excepted. Now when all things are made subject to Him, then the Son Himself will also be subject to Him who put all things under Him that God may be all in all.[25]**

Time is not the guiding force in the plan of God. In fact, time is not a factor nor does it concern the Triune God. His plan is to redeem a fallen mankind back unto Himself in an intimate and loving relationship which will last for all eternity. We, the Lord's believers, will be complete in Him.[26]

The predestination that I am advocating is that the plan is predestined. We as individuals are not necessarily predestined in the sense that most reformed adherents

---

[24] Psalms 8:6
[25] 1 Corinthians 15:23-28
[26] Colossians 2: 9-10

would maintain. I would maintain a difference between a global predestination or determinism and a local or individual predestination.

Our God is an awesome God. He is because He is. He needs nothing or no one for His existence. He is not contingent upon anything or anyone. Before creation, He was complete within Himself, within the Triune Godhead. Being of such a nature, we must hold and maintain that His grace is sufficient. Grace, the Greek word *charis,* simply means gift. How could any gift from an infinite and omniscient God not be sufficient unto its purpose? When we refer to redemption and salvation of a fallen mankind back to a holy God we must know and accept that the gift to accomplish this action from God in the form of God the Son must be sufficient. His grace is sufficient for this need through His Son, Jesus the Christ:

> **For in Him dwells all the fullness of the Godhead bodily; and you are complete in Him, who is the head of all principality and power. . .Having disarmed principalities and powers. He made a public spectacle of them, triumphing over them in it. . .which are a shadow of things to come, but the substance is of Christ.**[27]

From the above Scripture and the preceding one from Paul's Corinthian letter, we find that according to God all things: His plan, His purpose, and His power, is demonstrated and will be fruited by the grace, the gift given by God. We find this gift to be in the person of the Lord

---

[27] The Epistle to the Colossians 2:9-10, 15, and 17.

Jesus Christ, God the Son. How could this gift, this grace of God not be sufficient and somehow lacking according to His purpose and plan?

To return to the plum of our paradigm, we have a plan that is predestined and we have a grace to accomplish the plan which must be sufficient. The plan and the gift is given and completed by a God who is both omniscient and eternal. He knows all and He is infinite.

A second position of our paradigm is that God is omniscient and eternal. He sees the beginning from the end. He sees all and knows all. His predestined plan of redemption is looked at through eyes both eternal and all-knowing.

His plan and His grace, for a time, are sheltered in a temporary shelter of mankind in mortality. This fact of the mortality of the recipients of His grace is a third position of our paradigm. These bodies in which we dwell are only for a time. We must be saved and redeemed while in these mortal and temporary bodies:

> . . .lest the light of the gospel of the glory of Christ, who is the image of God should shine of them. For we do not preach ourselves, but Christ Jesus the Lord, and ourselves your bondservants for Jesus' sake. For it is the God who commanded light to shine out of darkness, who has shone in our hearts to give the light of the knowledge of the glory of God in the face of Jesus Christ. But we have this treasure in earthen vessels that the excellence of

the power may be of God and not of us. We are hard pressed on every side, yet not crushed; we are perplexed, but not in despair; persecuted, but not forsaken; struck down, but not destroyed-always carrying about in the body the dying of the Lord Jesus, that the life of Jesus also may be manifested in our body. For we who live are always delivered to death for Jesus' sake, that the life of Jesus also may be manifested in our mortal flesh. So then death is working in us, but life in you . . . knowing the He who raised up the Lord Jesus will also raise us up with Jesus, and will present us with you. For all things are for your sakes, that grace, having spread through the many, may cause thanksgiving to abound to the glory of God. Therefore we do not lose heart. Even though our outward man is perishing, yet the inward man is being renewed day by day. For our light affliction, which is but for a moment, is working for us a far more exceeding and eternal weight of glory, while we do not look at the things which are seen, but at the things which are not seen. For the things which are seen are temporary, but the things which are not seen are eternal. For we know that if our earthly house, this tent, is destroyed, we have a building from God, a house not made with hands eternal in the heavens.[28]

That most precious gift from God now resides, when a person is a believer, in a mortal, fallible, someday to die human vessel. This happenstance is necessary in order to

[28] 2 Corinthians 4:4-5:1

demonstrate that it is grace, a gift of God and not anything or method that we could accomplish within ourselves. His plan, His grace resides for a temporary and momentary speck of time within what we call mortal life. The Apostle Paul through the inspiration of God the Spirit in this translation calls it an earthen vessel. How flawed and transitory are our vessels to hold His grace.

A fourth position of our paradigm will be comfortable to those of the Arminian bent, but annoying to those of a more Augustinian or Calvinistic slant. Can a person lose their salvation? We, on both sides raise our hackles and hairs and stiffen our spines in entrenchment. I ask us all to take a deep proverbial breath for just a moment. Let us consider the Greek word: *apostasia.* It is the word from which we derive the English word: apostasy. It is a direct word. It means to depart. The modern word has a much more limited meaning and much more negative in scope. The word just means: to depart. We achieve this word from the two parts of the original Greek meaning: *apo* = away and *stasis* = stand. I, with my simple mind maintain that the word means: to stand away or to depart. The more limited definition comes from those who departed from the faith or have left the faith. My point in all of this is to demonstrate that one must have been somewhere to have left. One must be in the room to then depart from the room. A person by definition cannot be an apostate and not have been a believer. I refer you to Paul's reference of Demas, a student and aide of Paul who had chosen this world and left Paul.[29] Others in this verse had left Paul, but

---

[29] 2 Timothy 4:10

Demas had chosen this world and his love for it. The pressure got hot and Demas got going.

I have heard and have been instructed that a Calvinist position would be that if a person became a back-slider and has left the faith, it is demonstrative of the fact that that person was never a true believer. I know they have to maintain that position to continue their staunch adherence to the position of election. Are they not violating what the word apostate or apostasy means? I did not use the word. Through the inspiration of the Holy Spirit, this is the word used in Scripture. Simply put, a person cannot leave the room of Christianity unless they first were in the room. One cannot depart or stand away from something unless they first were someplace or were first standing someplace. A person with an opposing view cannot hold the person left the room, but really was not in the room. It violates the meaning of the word. We must not change the meaning of the word in order to maintain our too frail position that has grown and morphed from a mortal earthen vessel. We do not see through omniscient and eternal eyes. We have not achieved.[30] We see through a class darkly.[31] We, sometime and someplace outside of this mortality will know as we are known.[32] We will see Him as He is for we will be like Him.[33] On this side of the river separating mortality and immortality, we are not yet there in our understanding. Someday, oh yes thank God someday, our earthen vessels will give way to be further clothed in His

---

[30] Philippians 3:13
[31] 1 Corinthians 13:12
[32] 1 Corinthians 13:12
[33] 1 John 3:2-3

holiness.[34] Then all of us, from Calvin to Arminius, from Augustine of Hippo to this so human and frail writer will know and see and be and will understand completely and fully His plan and His grace and His purpose of redemption and His free-will given to frail mortals freely.

Allow me to reiterate our paradigm. The plan is predestined by God. He sees all and knows all. His grace must and is sufficient. He is eternal. He hides the treasure of His grace, His salvation and redemption within earthen vessels. Vessels must carry His grace though frail and fallible on this side of the river of mortality. He has given to us free-will and some may choose to leave and depart the room of His salvation and be as Demas and others of that same ilk.

ELECTION

The word 'election' is bantered and thrown about by both sides of this issue concerning predestination and free-will. I will offer my definition of the concept of election. I totally believe in election, but I feel that the Predestinarian side of the argument has seized this term and has limited its meaning. They have many Scriptures concerning election and they are correct in that the Lord has and must call us to come to be saved. They forget or ignore in a sort of myopia the very free-will given by the Lord to facilitate and allow for the intimate love relationship between Creator and His creation. Election and free-will are not exclusive of one another, but in fact are necessary components of the grace/faith dynamic. The reformed

---

[34] 2 Corinthians 5:2-5

Predestinarian adherent has done this to other terms such as 'reformed' and 'predestination'. Now they have limited their uses to their side of the discussion. Even their very use has come to imply a Calvinist point of view. Many on this side of the issue use the term double election to mean that there are those who are destined to be saved and the rest are destined to be lost and this election has occurred before time and mortality. I believe that we are elected by the Lord to be saved. The 'whosoever'[35] when applied to those in mortality says to me that all are elected to be saved, but most will deny the election.

I think of the word election as it might apply to a political election. A certain person may be elected to an office by a majority of the voters, but that person still must accept the election. I believe that the efficacy of the finished work of the cross and the resurrection of the Lord is sufficient and complete for all of the people whenever and wherever. How could the Lord and His passion and resurrection not be sufficient? Most in mortality will decide to reject the free gift of the Lord and promote themselves to be their own god. They have rejected the election of God for their own self-importance and self-absorption.

Many will say and allege that my defining of terms is simplistic and myopic. However we view and define terms, they must be brought into harmony and accord with Scripture. I believe and maintain that across the entire breadth and depth of the Holy bible my given definition of

---

[35] Romans 10:13, 2 Corinth. 5:14-15, 2 Peter 3:9, John 3:16, 1 Timothy 2:3

the election is consistent throughout the Word. Election is not an either/or, but a both/and situation.

A person's point of view one way or the other concerning this hot button topic must account for the sufficiency of the Lord's grace and His free-will gift to His creation to allow for the intimate love relationship between Creator and creation. Election by the Lord and a person's right of free-will to discard and not accept that election is not mutually exclusive. It is the given plan to a fallen creation by a loving God to facilitate the opportunity of souls to be reconciled back to God.

CROSSING A RIVER

I recall a story or parable given by a teacher that I have listened to and have learned much from over the many years that I have sat under his teaching ministry.[36] It is a story of a river and a person travelling across from one bank to the other. When our traveler first entered the cold and murky waters, he had to navigate whatever obstacles he may find within the stream. He had to side step the rocks and the boulders. He had to balance himself from the differences and changes of current. He had to elude any debris of sticks and limbs that may float in his way. The point is that during his crossing of the river the traveler had to decide many things. In many ways and at many times, he had to make a decision which might have altered his course or may have caused hurt or increase his changes of both failure and success in his journey. On the first side of the waters and during the crossing, our traveler can see the

---

[36] Mr. Les Feldick, Through the Bible Ministry, Tulsa, Oklahoma.

decisions in the process of the journey. When, upon reaching the far side of the river he would stand on the far shore and gaze back at the river all he could see was the placid and smooth river. The rocks and eddies and the perilous currents and the debris have smoothed due the distance and success of the traveler having reached the far shore.

Our journey through this life is much like the traveler in the above short parable. One this side of eternity and within our mortal walk we must wade into the cold and murky waters of mortal life. We shudder due the frigid nature of the cold waters soaking us with its torrents and temperature. We fight the eddy and the currents which seek to knock us from our feet and submerge us under the current. We feel the rocks and limbs and we must hold our ground or move around and about them while keeping our sold footage and security of purpose. We must take the one step after the other never forgetting our purpose and goal. Our goal is the far bank. Our goal is yonder shore. To reach the far shore we must first transverse and cross the river. Someday and someday soon we will reach that distant shore. We will lay down the mortality of life and lay it down for the eternality of our presence with the Lord.

When we are on the far shore and are present with the Lord and we are consumed and completed by Him, we will see that the passing of the river of mortality was due His peace and grace. We will look back at the river and see only the placid and calmness with which He has guided and directed us. We will see that our crossing the river was only due to Him and not due to anything we could have worked to accomplish.

Any parable or example can only partially direct us to His truth. We write and read while we are in the river. We are mortal. We are fallible. Any understanding we offer must always be seen in this light of frailty and partiality. As the Apostle Paul wrote, "We see in the mirror dimly."[37] My primary point which I wish to share is that while we are discussing our trek through this life we must remember that what we describe depends on one's point of view and his perspective. I would maintain that the Arminian and Free-will adherent is seeing the trek through mortality. He sees the choices and the rocks and the currents while travelling through and over the expanse and reaching out for the far shore. He has not attained that shore yet. He sees what Jacob Arminius described as contingencies or choices of life and what others have described as exercises of our Free-will.

The Calvinist or the Predestinarian or the Lutheran sees and describes the journey from the point of view of the far shore. The traveler is there and has achieved and stands safe in the far shore. His perspective is one of eternality and he sees through the lens of the Lord in His omniscience and eternality, His grace. When we are with the Lord for eternity, our salvation will work backwards, so to speak, and it will be as if we have always been elected by and for and through the Lord's grace. Conversely, the unregenerated person who enters eternity and has chosen his or hers own selfish desires and denies the Lord and His salvation will have his destruction work backwards until it will be that the

---

[37] 1 Corinthians 13:12.

sinner was always elected for perdition apart and away from the Lord. This salvation and this absence of salvation are and should be viewed from an eternal point of view when we here in this mortality talk of the Calvinist concepts of double election and predestination.

Throughout this work, I will maintain that the Arminian or Free-will disciple sees the trek and the mortal nature of the Christian life while the Predestinarian sees the accomplished goal from a grace perspective. This is not any either/or, but rather is a both/and situation. It is a perspective of the compatibilist.

The Free-will adherent sees through the eyes of faith. By this term faith, I mean what or who the believer believes to be true. It is his faith enhanced by the grace of God. The Predestinarian is seeing and defining his position through the lens of the grace of God. I believe that the Christian walk is an interaction between the sufficient grace of God and the faith of the believer. I believe to be saved a person must believe and have faith and believe to be true, in this Age of Grace the death, burial, and resurrection of the Lord Jesus Christ.[38] This death, burial, and resurrection of our Lord and Savior Jesus Christ, God the Son is the demonstrative gift, grace of the Triune God. This is His demonstration of love to us as believer.[39]

In conclusion to this little parable, during our mortal journey we see the choices and works we make and do

---

[38] 1 Corinthians 15:1-4. This is the Gospel message given for this Age of Grace.

[39] Romans 5:8.

crossing the river of life. When we are on the far shore, we look back and see the smoothness of the river and how the Lord has done the work allowing and enabling us to cross into His presence. It is His grace, His gift, His everything and we must have faith in, believe in, and trust as true His most precious gift who is He Himself.

REDEMPTION

Now He who searches the hearts knows what the mind of the Spirit is, because He makes intercession for the saints according to the will of God. And we know that all things work together for good to those who love God, to those who are the called according to His purpose. For whom He foreknew, He also predestined to be conformed to the image of His Son, that He might be the first born among many Brethren. Moreover whom He predestined, these He also called; whom He called, these He also Justified; and whom He justified, these He also glorified. What then shall we say to these things? If God is for us, who can be against us?[40]

We are slaves lost and away from the Lord. That is our lot and our burden. Some will hear the call of the Holy Spirit and come to accept the Lord. The creation He foreknew is each and every one of us. The plan He predestined is to allow the opportunity for those who accept His election to be conformed to the image of His Son. The plan found its completion in the efficacy of the death

---

[40] Romans 8:27-31.

and burial and resurrection of the Lord at Calvary during this age of Grace. We are called. Once called we cast off the sins of the fallen and we put off more and more this corrupted world. We must become like He is. We must put on the mind of Christ. We must become more and more chaste as the future Bride of Christ. This is truly what sanctification is to the believer. The process of changing our form to conform by transforming our form into His form is what this life in Christ is in our mortality. We become more and more like Him. In our time on this side of the river of mortality, He considers us just and justified for He is the justifier.[41] Someday however we will cross this hard river of mortality and be glorified. Then and only then we will be complete in Him[42] and the process of sanctification will have its completion and we will be holy as He is Holy.[43] We are commanded to be holy and we will be when we see Him as He is and we will be like He is.[44]

Look at this cycle of redemption from the end to the beginning of the above mentioned verses. The believer will someday be glorified. This will happen at death when we cross the river of mortality and reside in the eternal. The believer to enter into the eternal must be considered just by the Justifier, the Lord. The believer to have that judicial rendering of justification by the Lord must first be called. The plan of the Lord to call folks unto salvation was predestined by the Triune God. The plan of Grace is found complete in the Passion and Resurrection of the Lord at

---

[41] Romans 2:16, Romans 3:24, 3:26
[42] Colossians 2:10
[43] 1 Peter 1:16
[44] 1 John 3:1-2

Calvary, the Passover and Unleavened Bread and Firstfruits. Of course the Lord foreknew each and every one of us. This is the nature of the omniscience of God. This cycle is the plan that works together for good if we love God.

OUR HARD LIFE

Our lives are burdened with the hard life. Many times we do not and cannot know the whys and the wherefores of our times and predicaments. We view the fires and adversities with reasonable reluctance and fear. However, we must look at our times and perils and difficulties in a different way when we are Christians. We must always keep in mind that this life, this time of mortality is one of a stage in our growth and not the final destination or product. This life is to change the Christian from who he is to whom the Lord Jesus Christ wishes him to become. We travel the path. We learn the truth. We live the life.[45] It is a different path than the one we walked before our conversion. It is a different and fuller truth than the truths we held before our conversion. It is a different life than the one we lived before our conversion. We have become slaves to His righteousness.[46] We are becoming new creatures.[47] We are becoming Christians or little Christs.

We now find ourselves as Christians in the forge of the sanctifying Holy Spirit. His purpose as a member of the Triune God is to guide and instruct us to reflect and become more and more like in resemblance and character and

---

[45] John 14:6
[46] Romans 6:18
[47] 2 Corinthians 5:17

image to the second member of the Triune God, the Lord Jesus Christ. We are to prepare ourselves to become more and more chaste awaiting that glorious time when we become the Lord's Bride.

Think of the olden days of the western America where we rode horses and drove wagons. A primary profession of those days was the blacksmith. I pondered concerning his craft. He had a forge and a hammer and an anvil and he would fashion many things that the folk found necessary. Think of it as he would take a piece of metal with no fashion of purpose, obstinate and stubborn and mold it into something of value and purpose. The smithy would put the metal in the fire of the forge and would heat and heat the metal until it would glow the red hue of heated metal just to begin the process. He would place the metal on the anvil and begin to beat and hit the piece of metal with the heavy hammer. Hit after hit. He would again reheat the metal in the forge. Then removing the metal, he would once again begin the process of the hitting and shaping the metal into whatever was its intended purpose. Perhaps a horseshoe or an axle for a wagon, or this or that would be the end product. Each tool or product began with the same process. The heating of an object. The beating of the smithy's hammer on the metal upon the anvil until the final product was forged and shaped and when the process was completed then the product was immersed in water and sealed to its use.

Our Christian life is much like the above story. When we have become Christians we do not know. We do not understand. We are not useful to the degree in which is necessary to be of complete use to the Lord. The Holy Spirit takes us through the hard fire of life. When the fires of life assail the Christian, it is in a different way than the non-Christian. The Holy Spirit takes hold of us and we find ourselves heated and under duress and stress. Then the Holy Spirit will take up in his mighty and divine hands His hammer of sanctification and begin to mold and shape use into someone fruitful and useful to the Church and to the Lord, the Head of the Church. This is the purpose of sanctification. This is the method of the Lord to change you and I to become a chaste bride. We, through this process cast off the dross and excess and obstinacy and stubbornness bit by bit with each strike of the holy hammer of God. This process may be painful to our mortal minds and willful spirits, but the Lord will have His way. His purpose will be done in our lives. The real purpose of this life is to make us to be presentable to a Holy and perfect God in eternity.

This life is but a stage, a preparation, and a time of trial and fire to mold and shape us to be more and more Christians or little Christs. The fire is hot. The hammer is hard. The anvil is unmoving and stern and strong, but we must remember it is His fire. It is His hammer. It is His anvil. He is the Smithy and it is His forge and it is His sanctification and process purposed on each believer.

The end result of this process of being molded more and more into His image is by the time we leave time and enter eternity we will be fit and ready to be complete in Him. Where we have begun in our Christian walk will one day be fruited and completed in Him. We will be an heir and a joint-heir with Him. Our form will have been transformed to conform to His form to paraphrase Romans 12:1-2. We must recall and remember that this life is but a stage, (re. 2 Corinthians Ch. 4). We are still in mortality and in time. We are still those earthen vessels in the process of being redeemed and made holy as He is holy. We still are clothed in the temporary tents of mortality and have not been clothed fully in His holiness which will occur as we step into eternity.

CONCLUDING THOUGHTS

I hope and pray that in the few short pages concerning this deep and complex subject I may have painted our wall of understanding in a coherent and succinct manner. The words above are, of course not meant to be exhaustive nor meant to be academic, but I believe I have covered our wall of understanding in an accumulative method. The points given above are offered as a bit of information offered by a lesser than adequate person. I believe and I mean this whole-heartedly that we swim the deep waters of truth with mill stones tied about our necks. We burden ourselves trying to fit the omnipotent, omnipresent, and omniscient Lord into the box of understanding of a mortal mind. It is my view that all denominations and doctrinal bents do this very thing. I believe and maintain that whatever our view we must cover the entire breadth of Scripture. We must not chisel away portions of Scripture which do not fit our presuppositions. We must not ignore portions of the Holy Bible which vary and go contrary to our sacred cows of traditions and heritage.

In our mortality, we clearly see we are subject and slave to our choices. We vary and alter our way and sidestep this or that in our walk. We choose for or against a particular thing or option. We move forward or retreat from this or that in our experiences. It seems we do all of the above with each waking and sleeping moment of our journey across the river of mortality. We see Jacob Arminius' doctrine of contingency. We could call this our choices subject to our given free-will. None-the-less, we know within and due our experience that this is the case. We must strive to hold on to His garment's hem and pray He helps us through this hard valley of life.

When we cross that river of mortality and we see Him face to face, so to speak, we shall see Him as He is. When we are in eternity, we shall be like He is. The river being behind us and crossed we now look back with His eyes and see that it was all about His grace. It was all about how He carried us through.

With eternal eyes and seeing through that prospective of eternity, we will know the reality of double election. His judgement and redemption, either accepted or rejected, will work backwards. The believer will be in a state where he or she always has been elected. If a person rejects the humanity and grace offered and already paid for through the death, burial, and resurrection of the Lord Jesus Christ, that same process will work backwards to demonstrate that that person will have always been lost and condemned to perdition. Either choice becomes and demonstrates the ultimate interaction of God's given grace which of course is sufficient and mankind's free-will which of course is necessary to fulfill and promote and accomplish the desire of the Lord to have a love relationship with His creation, humankind.

In the Gospel of St. Mathew chapter 22:34-40, the Lord was asked what was the great commandment. He responded by saying there were two. The first and greatest was to love God. The second was like unto it in that we the creation love each other. The Lord states that all the Law and the Prophets hang upon these two laws. Let us ponder a bit on this portion of Scripture. Loving God depicts a verticality of direction. Humankind upwardly is loving God and of course God downwardly in reciprocity is loving us. This is grace. He loves us in a gift and we in return love Him. The real meaning of *eucharistia,* the Eucharist, our communion is to display the demonstration of His grace and our reciprocity of that grace back to Him. It is vertical. The second is like the first in that it is love.   It is the demonstration of love horizontally between the creation and others of the creation. It is a choice of the servant to be serving. It is the choice of the loved to love. It is the choice of the recipient of mercy to be merciful. It is the horizontal manifestation that springs from the vertical manifestation of His grace.

In the fruition of the two directions we have received a verbal picture of the Cross. All we are and can be is fruited and finished in the Gospel message of God. All grace points us to the Cross and our faith directs us both vertically to Him and horizontally to creation to be His hands and feet. We are to be His church, *kuriakos* in the Greek, pertaining and relating to the Lord.

I hope and trust and pray that this little essay may help some along the way to see that the question of eternal security, predestinarianism and free-will is not either/or, but is both/and in reality. The plan is from the very foundation of the world and predestined by the eternal omniscient Lord. His grace is sufficient. It must be. How could an all-knowing God be insufficient in anything He would do or accomplish? This grace during our mortality is held and dwells within earthen and flawed vessels. In our infirmity, His strength is made evident to paraphrase 2 Corinthians Ch. 12. His strength and our weakness during our mortality make necessary the sufficiency of His grace during our walk on this side of mortality and crossing that river to reach the far shore. We err and sin and fall short, but He loves us and spreads His grace over us to see us through this stage and life until we are home and complete with Him. There are those who, however decide to walk away from the Lord and decide to be apostate. Demas from the Scripture and Joseph Stalin are two examples. They loved this world more than they loved the Lord. They ripped the Holy Spirit from their very being and made themselves their own gods. They are lost forever deciding to choose the mortal in lieu of the immortal. They loved their lives in lieu of loving the Lord and His offered gift of salvation. Walk His path. Choose His way. Learn His truth. Live His life. In the end when we see Him as He is and we will be like He is, He will say, "My good and faithful servant."[48]

---

[48] Mathew 25:21, 23

APPENDIX ONE: DIAGRAMS

THE TABLE OF SALVATION

GRACE

THE GOSPEL

I Cor. 15:1-4

FAITH

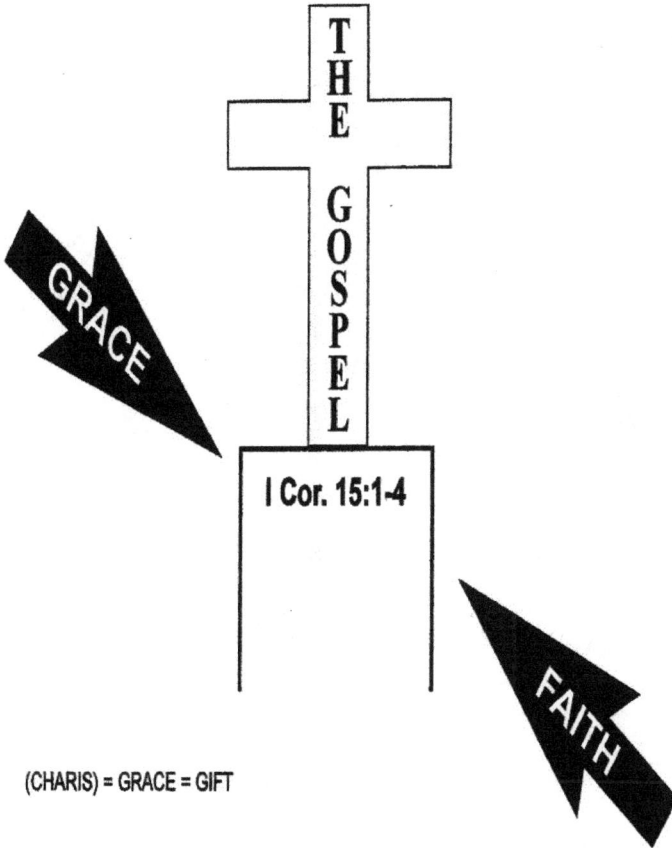

(CHARIS) = GRACE = GIFT

(PISTIS) = FAITH, BELIEF, TRUST

CHARIS (Given to us)

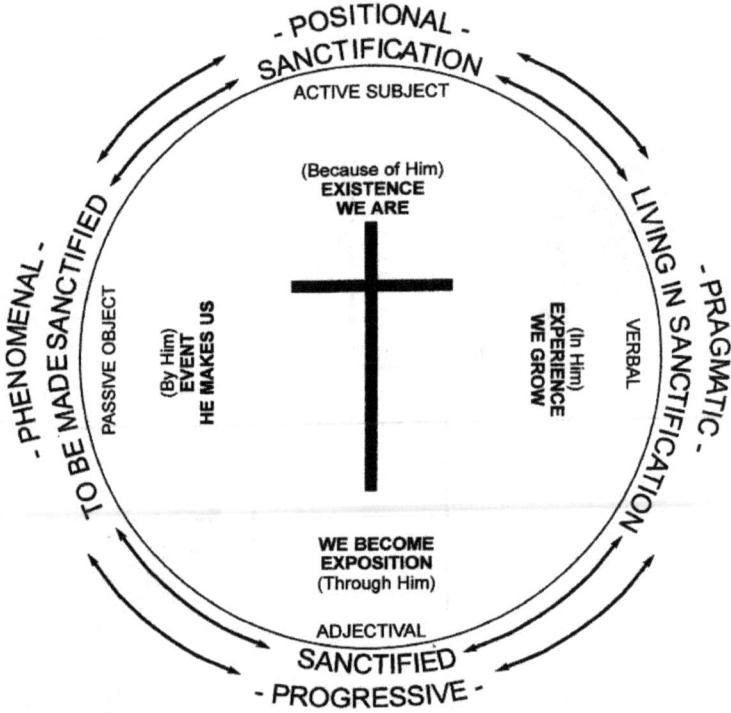

THE CYCLE OF SANCTIFICATION

- POSITIONAL -
SANCTIFICATION
ACTIVE SUBJECT

- PHENOMENAL -
TO BE MADE SANCTIFIED
PASSIVE OBJECT

- PRAGMATIC -
LIVING IN SANCTIFICATION
VERBAL

(Because of Him)
**EXISTENCE
WE ARE**

(By Him)
**EVENT
HE MAKES US**

(In Him)
**EXPERIENCE
WE GROW**

**WE BECOME
EXPOSITION**
(Through Him)

ADJECTIVAL
SANCTIFIED
- PROGRESSIVE -

A LANGUAGE EVENT OF ETERNAL REALITY FROM GOD

(re.: LEGO/LOGOS ➤ A COMMUNICATION FROM GOD
➤ AN ACT OF GRACE

SUBJECTIVE = US   OBJECTIVE = GOD   (An imitation of God in us)

HEB. 2:10-11
JUDE 1
1 COR. 1:2
POSITIONAL

ACTS 20:32, 26:18
1 COR. 6:11
HEB. 10:14
EPH. 5:26

1 COR. 1:30
1 TH. 5:23
HEB. 10:10

PHENOMENAL
2 TH. 2:13
ROM. 15:16

PRAGMATIC
ROM. 6:19, 21

HEB. 9:11-15
HEB. 13:12

HEB. 12:14
1 PE. 3:15
1 PE. 1:2
1 TH. 4:3-4
JOHN 17:17-19

PROGRESSIVE
1 PE. 2:9
1 TH. 4:7

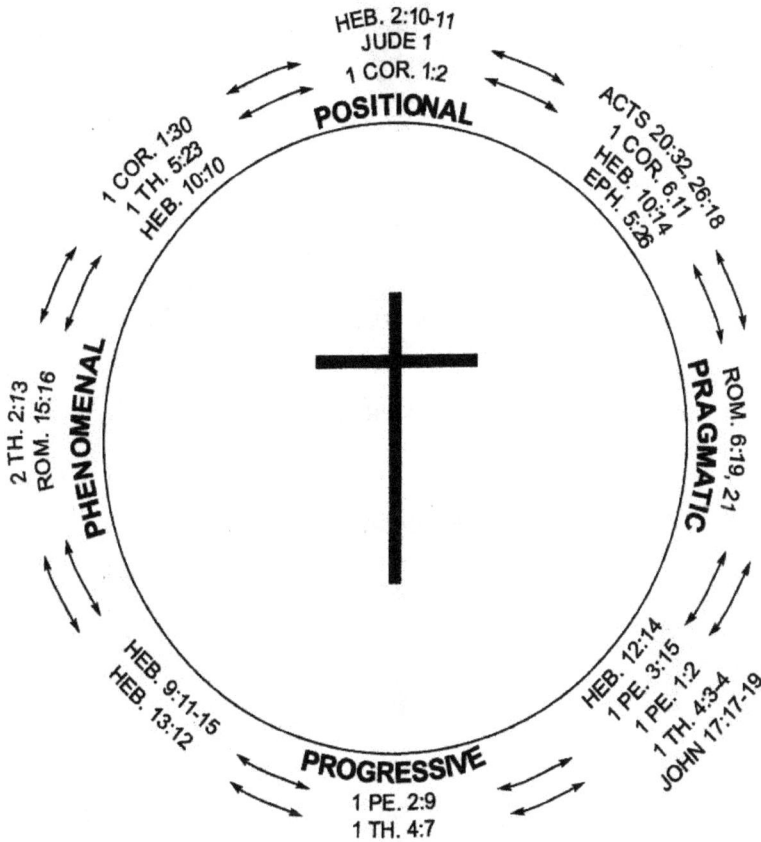

AN INTERACTIVE SANCTIFICATION

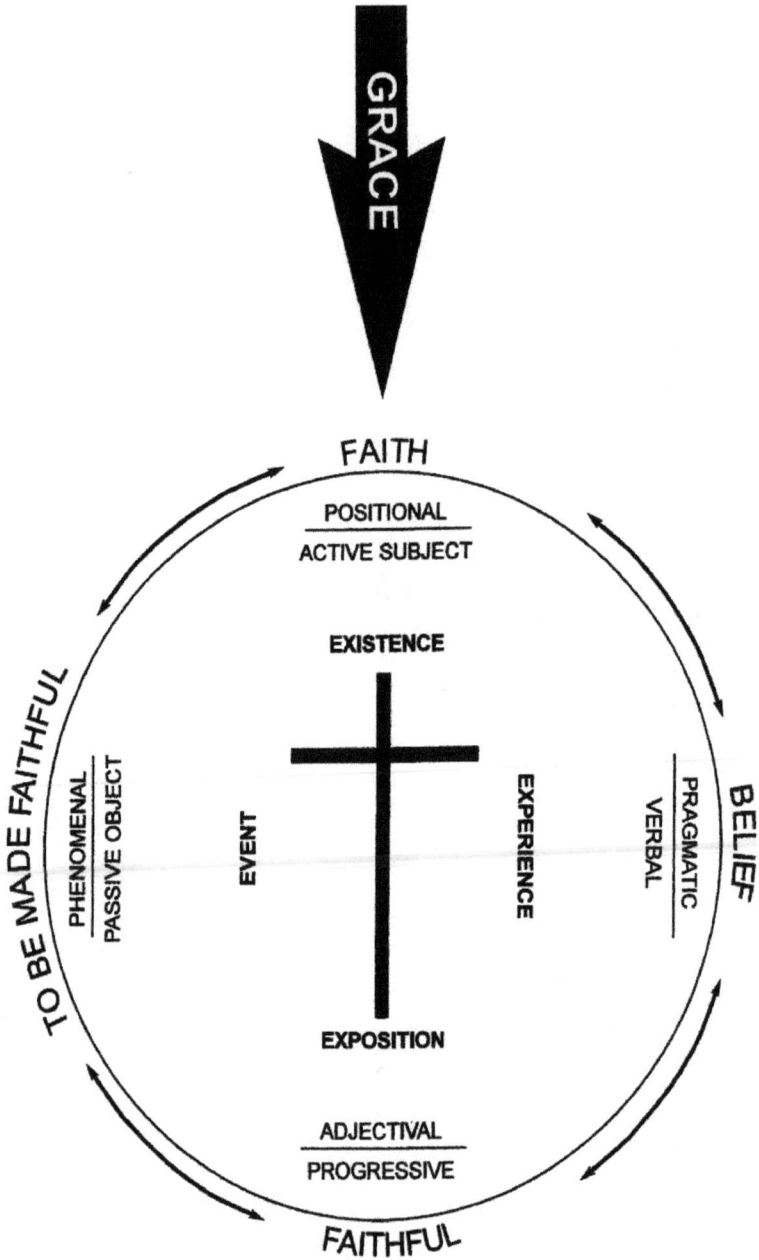

THE CYCLE OF FAITH   2 TIMOTHY 3:14-15

OUR IMITATION OF CHRIST

WE LOVE GOD

OUR GRACE AGAIN
WE LOVE
WE ARE MERCIFUL

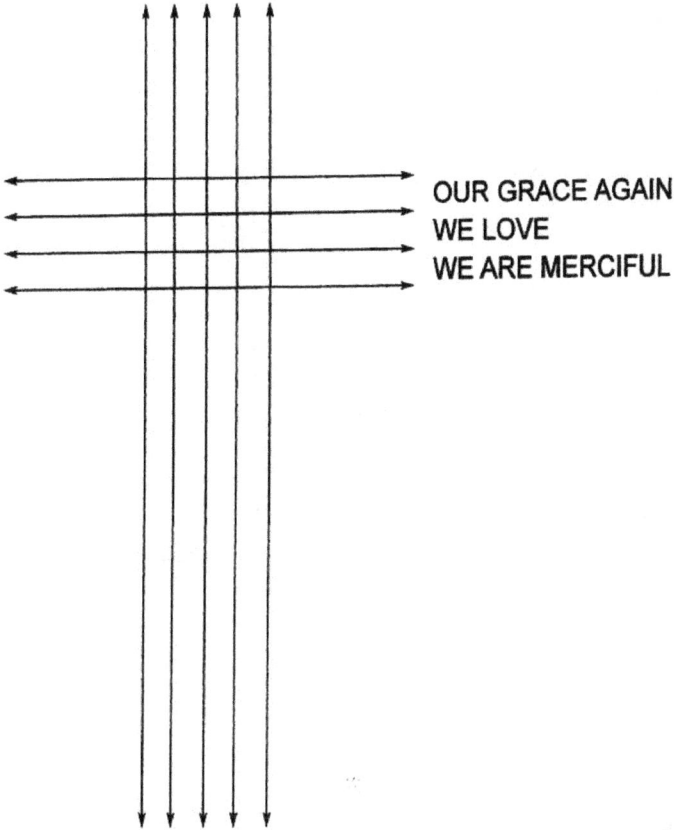

GOD'S
LOVE, MERCY, GRACE

MATTHEW 22:37-40

OUR IMITATION OF CHRIST

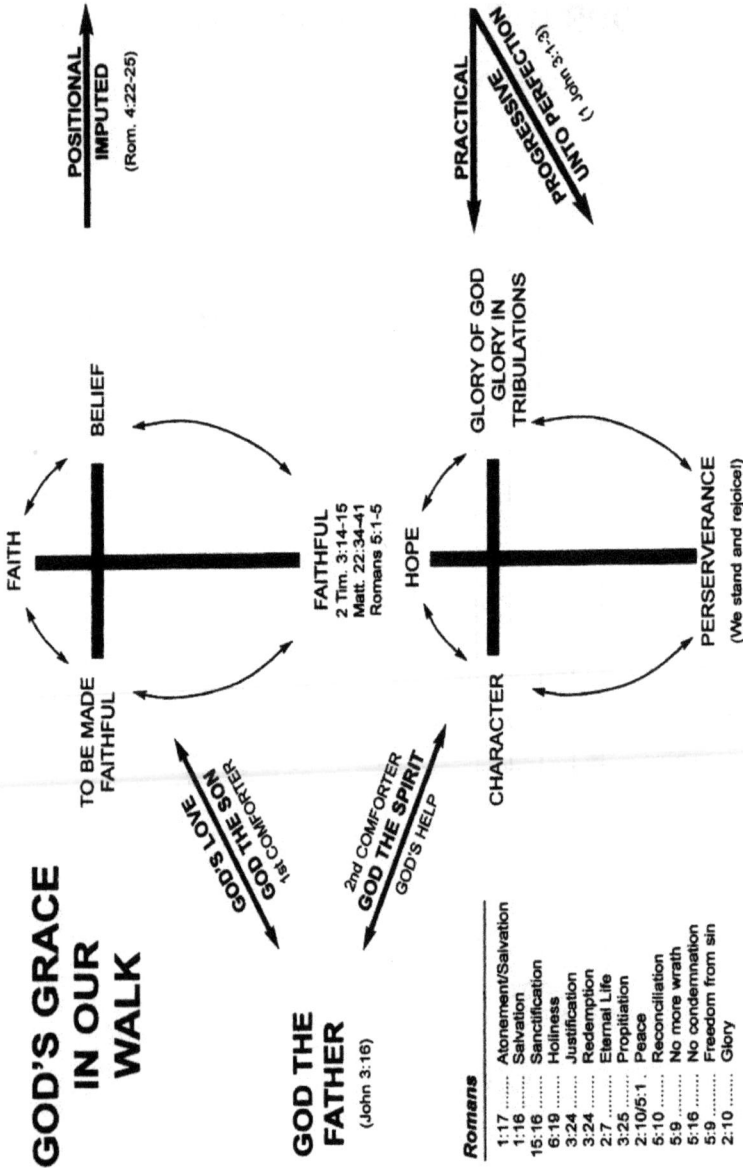

POSITIONAL
IMPUTED
(Rom. 4:22-25)

PRACTICAL

PROGRESSIVE

UNTO PERFECTION (1 John 3:1-3)

BELIEF

FAITH

TO BE MADE FAITHFUL

FAITHFUL
2 Tim. 3:14-15
Matt. 22:34-41
Romans 5:1-5

HOPE

GLORY OF GOD
GLORY IN TRIBULATIONS

PERSERVERANCE
(We stand and rejoice!)

CHARACTER

GOD'S LOVE
GOD THE SON
1st COMFORTER

2nd COMFORTER
GOD THE SPIRIT
GOD'S HELP

GOD'S GRACE IN OUR WALK

GOD THE FATHER
(John 3:16)

Romans

1:17	Atonement/Salvation
1:16	Salvation
15:16	Sanctification
6:19	Holiness
3:24	Justification
3:24	Redemption
2:7	Eternal Life
3:25	Propitiation
2:10/5:1	Peace
5:10	Reconciliation
5:9	No more wrath
5:16	No condemnation
5:9	Freedom from sin
2:10	Glory

The Prophetic Calendar

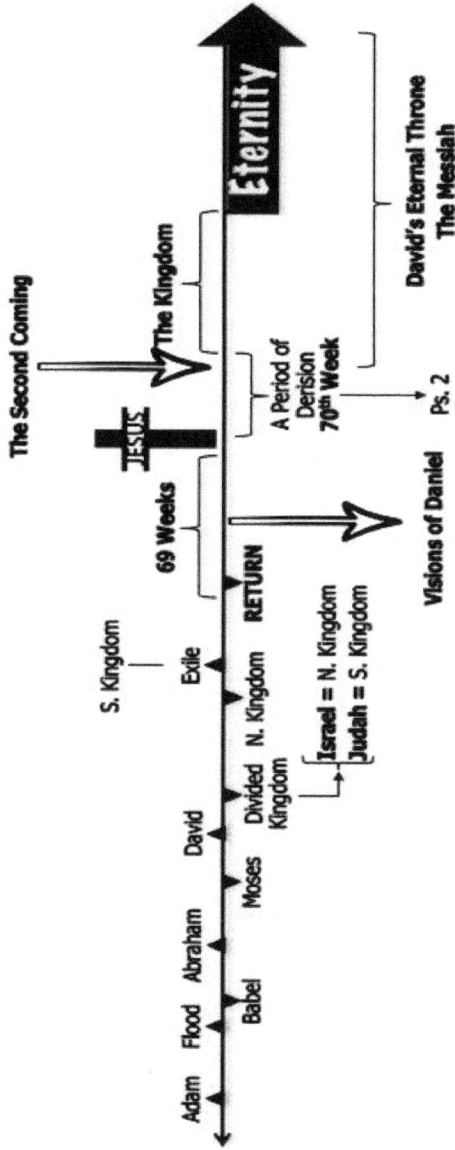

Adam Flood Abraham Moses David Divided Kingdom N. Kingdom Exile RETURN

Babel

S. Kingdom

Israel = N. Kingdom
Judah = S. Kingdom

69 Weeks

JESUS

The Second Coming

The Kingdom

A Period of Derision
70th Week

Eternity

Visions of Daniel

Ps. 2

David's Eternal Throne
The Messiah

The Dispensation of Grace

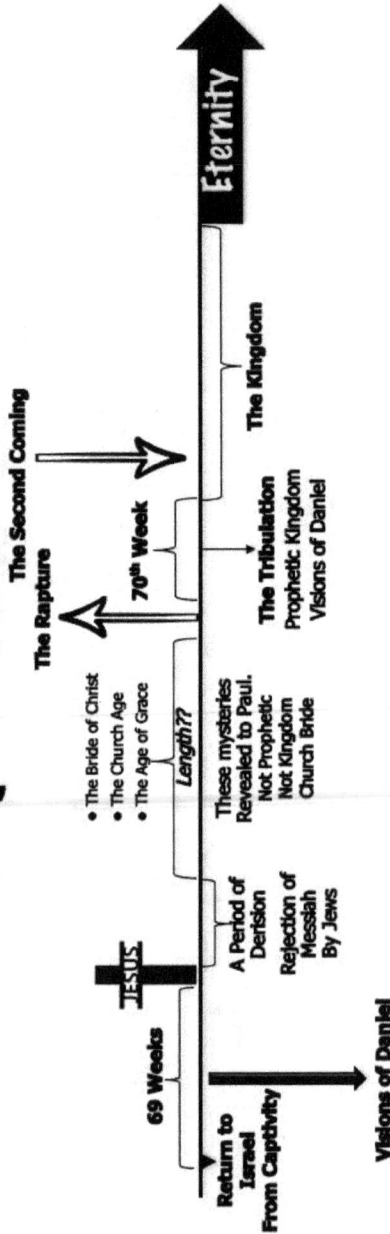

Eternity

The Second Coming

The Rapture

70th Week

The Kingdom

• The Bride of Christ
• The Church Age
• The Age of Grace

Length??

These mysteries
Revealed to Paul.
Not Prophetic
Not Kingdom
Church Bride

The Tribulation
Prophetic Kingdom
Visions of Daniel

A Period of
Derision
Rejection of
Messiah
By Jews

JESUS

69 Weeks

Return to
Israel
From Captivity

Visions of Daniel

• Galatians 4:4-5
• 1 Corinthians 15: 23-28
• Romans 8:29
• 1 Thessalonians 4:13-18

The High Holy Days

Leviticus 23 – 7 Feasts
1 MACC - Hanukkah

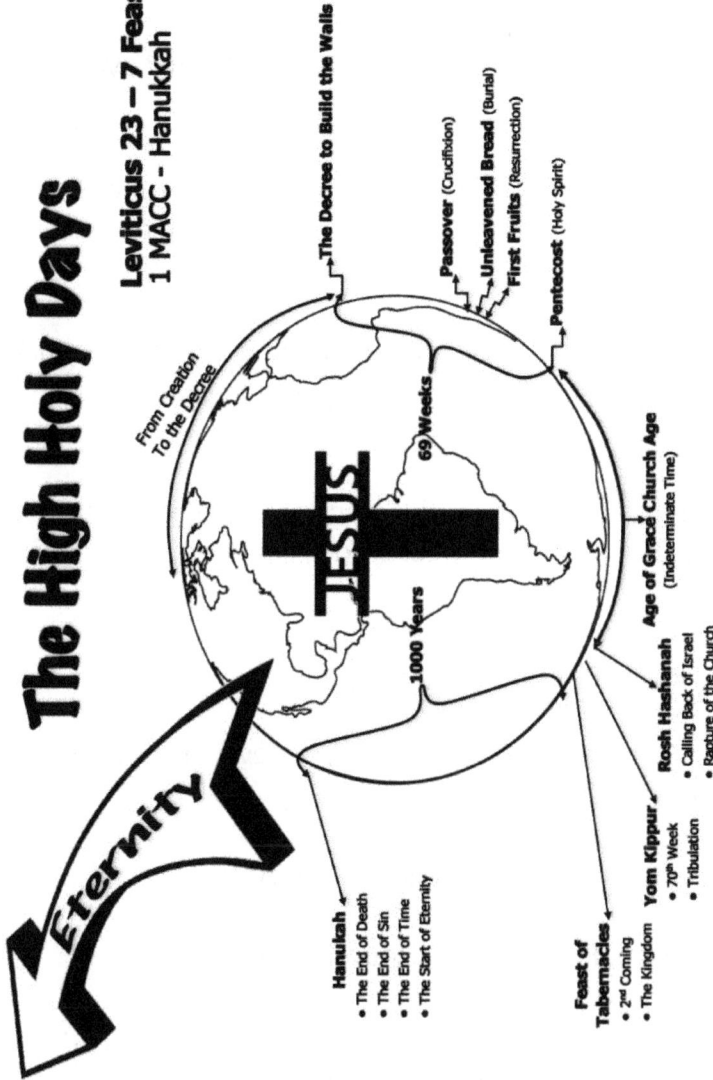

The Decree to Build the Walls

From Creation
To the Decree

Passover (Crucifixion)

Unleavened Bread (Burial)

First Fruits (Resurrection)

Pentecost (Holy Spirit)

JESUS

69 Weeks

1000 Years

Age of Grace Church Age
(Indeterminate Time)

Eternity

Hanukkah
• The End of Death
• The End of Sin
• The End of Time
• The Start of Eternity

Feast of Tabernacles
• 2nd Coming
• The Kingdom

Yom Kippur
• 70th Week
• Tribulation

Rosh Hashanah
• Calling Back of Israel
• Rapture of the Church

LIST OF WORKS CITED

Clarke, David E. Rev., "Concerning the Christ," FWB Publishing. c. 2011.

Green, Keith and Todd Fishkind and Randy Stonehill, "Your Love Broke Through," April Music, Inc. / King of Hearts Publishing (ASCAP) c. 1976, 1977.

Gaither, Gloria words and Jean Sibelius music, "I Then Shall Live," c. Warner/Chappell Music, Inc. Universal Music Publishing Group.

Heber, Reginald, lyrics 1826 and John B. Dykes, music 1861, "Holy, Holy, Holy Lord God Almighty".

Lewis, Clives Staples, "Mere Christianity," c. 1980, C.S. Lewis Pte. Ltd.

Mallard, "I Can Only Imagine," Simpleville Music (ASCAP). C. 2001,2002

The New King James Version of the Holy Bible

Thompson, Francis, "The Hound of Heaven," McCracken Press, c. 1993.

Updike, John, "Seven Stanzas at Easter," c. 1961, John Updike. Reprinted by Dr. John W. Montgomery, "The Suicide of Christian Theology," Newburgh, Indiana: Trinity Press, c. 1970.

Weeks, The Rev. Canon Philip El P. with Hugh W. Kaiser, "Non Nobis, Domine!" c. Barnabas Ministries, Inc.